Top Ten Tips

A Survival Guide for Families with Children on the Autism Spectrum

Teresa A. Cardon, M.A., CCC-SLP

Foreword by Kristi Sakai

©2008 Autism Asperger Publishing Company
P. O. Box 23173
Shawnee Mission, Kansas 66283-0173
www.asperger.net • 877-288-8254

Publisher's Cataloging-in-Publication

Cardon, Teresa A.
  Top ten tips : a survival guide for families with children on the autism spectrum / Teresa A. Cardon. -- 1st ed. -- Shawnee Mission, Kan. : Autism Asperger Pub. Co., 2008.

    p. ; cm.
    ISBN: 978-1-934575-30-7
    LCCN: 2008935432
    Includes bibliographical references.

    1. Autistic children--Family relationships. 2. Autistic children--Care. 3. Autism--Patients--Family relationships. 4. Asperger's syndrome--Patients--Family relationships. 5. Parents of autistic children--Handbooks, manuals, etc. I. Title. II. Title: Survival guide for families with children on the autism spectrum.
    RJ506.A9 C378 2008   2008935432
    649/.154--dc22   0809

This book is designed in Accent and Myriad.

Printed in the United States of America.

Acknowledgments

This book has been a labor of love. I am humbled by the willingness of so many people to jump right in and help out. I know you all lead busy lives and your effort to support our families is incredible. My sincerest appreciation to all of you!

I would be remiss if I didn't thank one person in particular. Cindy, you are an amazing mother and cherished friend, and I am one of your biggest fans. Thank you for inviting me on Eric's journey! Your support and assistance with this book has been phenomenal. I don't think I could have done it without you. Your unique perspective and persistent collection of tips have made many great additions to this book. Thank you!

And of course, my incredible family – Craig, Rylee and Breelyn. I am blessed to have your support and love every day. I couldn't do this if you weren't so understanding and patient with me! Thank you for everything, great and small. My heart to you!

– T.A.C.

Contributors

Diane Adreon – Associate director of the University of Miami/ Nova Southeastern University Center for Autism & Related Disabilities. Diane is the co-author of *Asperger Syndrome and Adolescence: Practical Solutions* and *Simple Strategies That Work! Helpful Hints for All Educators of Students with Asperger Syndrome, High-Functioning Autism, and Related Disabilities*.

Chari Alvarez-Reynolds – Mother of a 4-year-old child with autism spectrum disorders.

Terri Anasagasti – Mother of a 3-1/2-year-old son with autism spectrum disorders and a 5-year-old neurotypical daughter.

Jamie Blunt – Mother of two boys, including a 5-year-old who is nonverbal and has autism spectrum disorders.

Becky Bornhoft – Mother of two children, including a 6-year-old son on the autism spectrum.

Jenny Clark Brack, OTR/L – Licensed pediatric occupational therapist. Works for Three Lakes Educational Cooperative and owns a pediatric therapy private practice, Jenny's Kids, Inc. Jenny is the author of *Learn to Move, Move to Learn: Sensorimotor Early Childhood Activity Themes* and *Sensory Processing Disorder: Simulations & Solutions for Parents, Teachers, and Therapists*.

Amy Bixler Coffin, M.S. – Education autism administrator for the Ohio Center for Autism and Low Incidence (OCALI). Amy is the co-author of *Out and About: Preparing Children with Autism Spectrum Disorders to Participate in Their Communities*.

Kari Dunn Buron – Recently retired after 33 years of working as a special education teacher in the public schools. Co-author of *The Incredible 5-Point Scale* and author of *When My Worries Get Too Big!, A "5" Could Make Me Lose Control,* and *A 5 Is Against the Law*; co-editor of *Learners on the Autism Spectrum: Preparing Highly Qualified Educators*.

Teresa Cardon, M.A. CCC-SLP – Speech language pathologist and faculty research associate, Arizona State University. Teresa is the author of *Let's Talk Emotions* and *Initiations and Interactions*.

Joan Clark – Speech/language pathologist, who has spent her career in the public school sector. Joan is the author of *Ann Drew Jackson* and *Jackson Whole Wyoming*.

Lynne Stern Feiges – Attorney, writer, and mother of two. Grew up with three brothers, two of whom are on the autism spectrum. Lynne is the co-author of *Sibling Stories: Reflections on Life with a Brother or Sister on the Autism Spectrum*.

Jennifer Frandsen, BSN, RN – Mother of a 6-year-old daughter with autism spectrum disorders.

Glenda Fuge, MS, OTR/L – Co-author of *Pathways to Play! Combining Sensory Integration and Integrated Play Groups*.

Tiffany Fullmer – Certified massage therapist and single mother of two children; has an adult brother with Asperger Syndrome.

Prather Harrell – Transformational life coach, mother of three children, including a 3-½-year-old with autism spectrum disorders.

Sharon Hayes – Co-founder of Phoenix HFA/Asperger Family Network.

Juliane Hillock, MAEd – Special education teacher, Mesa Public Schools, Mesa, Arizona.

Jill Hudson, MS, CCLS – Certified child life specialist. Currently National State and Community Partnerships, the Ohio Center for Autism and Low Incidence (OCALI). Jill is the co-author of *Out and About: Preparing Children with Autism Spectrum Disorders to Participate in Their Communities* and author of *Prescription for Success: Supporting Children with Autism Spectrum Disorders in the Medical Environment* and *Cabins, Canoes and Campfires: Guidelines for Establishing a Camp for Children with Autism Spectrum Disorders*.

Renata Irving – Educator, activist and mother of two teens, one with autism spectrum disorders.

Kathryn Jolley – Mother of one son, and three daughters, one of whom has an autism spectrum disorder.

Joanna Keating-Velasco – Instructional aide (independence facilitator) in programs for children, teens and adults with autism. Joanna is the author of *A Is for Autism, F Is for Friend* and *In His Shoes.*

Lisa Keegan – Mother of a 10-year-old girl with autism spectrum disorders and a 7-year-old son.

Paula Kluth, Ph.D. – Consultant, teacher, author, advocate and independent scholar. Paula is the author of *You're Going to Love This Kid! Teaching Students with Autism in the Inclusive Classroom.*

Anthony Koutsoftas, M.S., CCC-SLP – Speech language pathologist in private practice.

Caroline Levine – Former teacher, currently writes for children, takes community college classes, and tutors children with autism. Carol is the author of *Jay Grows an Alien*.

Lisa Lieberman, MSW – Clinical social worker doing psychotherapy in private practice. Lisa's son Jordan is a high school senior and a delightful young man with autism. Lisa is the author of *A "Stranger" Among Us: Hiring In-Home Support for a Child with Autism Spectrum Disorders or Other Neurological Differences*.

Hunter Manasco – Speech language pathologist specializing in autism and neurogenic communication disorders. He is pursuing a Ph.D. at the University of South Alabama. Hunter is the author of *The Way to A: Empowering Children with Autism Spectrum and Other Neurological Disorders to Monitor and Replace Aggression and Tantrum Behavior*.

Heather McCracken – Mother of three children, one of whom is diagnosed with autism spectrum disorders. Heather is the creator of the Friend 2 Friend model and founder and executive director of the Friend 2 Friend Social Learning Society. She is also the author of *That's What's Different About Me! Helping Children Understand Autism Spectrum Disorders*.

Amy Misencik – Mother of a 5-year-old child with autism spectrum disorders.

Susan Morris – RN and mother of three boys, one with autism spectrum disorders.

Brenda Smith Myles, Ph.D. – Consultant with the Ziggurat Group. Recipient of the 2004 Autism Society of America's Outstanding Professional Award and the 2006 Princeton Fellowship Award. She has written and co-authored numerous articles and books on Asperger Syndrome and autism, including *Asperger Syndrome and Difficult Moments, Asperger Syndrome and Adolescents, The Hidden Curriculum,* and *Children and Youth With Asperger Syndrome: Strategies for Success in Inclusive Settings*.

Jeanine Nesvik – Swim instructor and interventionist for children with autism spectrum disorders.

Cindy O'Dell – Mother of three boys, one of whom has autism spectrum disorders.

Michelle Pomeroy – Advocate and dedicated aunt of three children with special needs, including autism spectrum disorders.

Holly Reycraft, Ma.Ed. – Mother of a 10-year-old with autism spectrum disorders. She has spent 9 years in a school system as special education counselor.

Kristi Sakai – Kristi lives on a farm in Oregon with her three children and husband, all of whom are on the autism spectrum. Kristi is the author of *Finding Our Way: Creating a Supportive Home and Community for the Asperger Syndrome Family*, which received the Autism Society of America's 2006 Literary Work of the Year in the Family Social category.

Josie Santomauro – Resides in Brisbane, Australia, and has a son with Asperger Syndrome. Josie is an internationally published author. She is the co-author of *Space Travelers: Developing Social Understanding, Social Competence and Social Skills for Students with AS, Autism and Other Social Cognitive Challenges; Pirates: An Early-Years Group Program for Developing Social Understanding and Social Competence for Children with Autism Spectrum and Related Disorders;* and *Asperger Download: A Guide to Help Teenage Males with Asperger Syndrome Trouble-Shoot.*

Stephen Shore, Ph.D. – Diagnosed with "atypical development with strong autistic tendencies," Stephen Shore was viewed as "too sick" to be treated on an outpatient basis and recommended for institutionalization. Stephen is a national and international presenter on autism and assistant professor at Adelphi University. Stephen is the author of *Beyond the Wall: Personal Experiences with Autism and Asperger Syndrome* and editor of *Ask and Tell: Self-Advocacy and Disclosure for People on the Autism Spectrum.*

Wallis A. Simpson – Mother of two boys, Jesse and Andrew. Andrew was diagnosed with an autism spectrum disorder when he was 4. The diagnosis was changed to Asperger Syndrome when he was 7. Wallis is the author of *My Andrew: Day-to-Day Living with a Child with an Autism Spectrum Disorder*.

Mindy Small, M.A. – Coordinator of autism services for Herbert G. Birch Services, Inc. Mindy is the author of *Everyday Solutions: A Practical Guide for Families of Children with Autism Spectrum Disorders.*

Melissa Van Hook – Mother of two boys with autism spectrum disorders and founding member and co-facilitator for E.V.A.N. – East Valley Autism Network.

Michele Walker – With a master's degree in applied educational psychology, Michele has been extensively involved in researching and providing developmental services for her own children as well as others in the community. Michele is the author of *BeeVisual's Choiceworks™ System.*

Pamela Wolfberg, Ph.D. – Associate professor of special education at San Francisco State University, where she developed an autism spectrum graduate program. Her current research and practice focus on supporting children with autism spectrum disorders in the areas of peer relations, play, childhood culture, and social inclusion. Pamela is the author of *Peer Play and the Autism Spectrum* and co-editor of *Learners on the Autism Spectrum: Preparing Highly Qualified Educators.*

Katie Wride – Mother of four children, one with autism spectrum disorders. Katie is an autism advocate.

Table of Contents

Foreword

Autism spectrum disorder (ASD) is complex. Theories and treatment options are varied, and many conflict with each other because even the experts don't always agree. When you add in that every individual is impacted *differently* by the characteristics of ASD, it is no wonder that it is sometimes an overwhelming prospect to understand how to help a specific child. Where are on earth do you even begin?

I've come to believe that regardless of what treatment options you choose, first and foremost you must assist the child's immediate needs in real life. This book offers diverse ideas that can be immediately implemented in addressing daily situations that we commonly face as parents and teachers of children with ASD.

When the oldest of my three children was initially diagnosed, there were few books available on the subject and it was extremely difficult to get a handle on exactly what this mysterious ASD was. Worse, there was a particular shortage of information when I hit the most common daily obstacles. How do we handle community outings and social situations? And even if we're brave enough to go out, how do we help our child endure tooth brushing and bathing beforehand? In frustration I often thought, "What do I DO?"

As my second, and then third, child was diagnosed a few years later, I found that almost an overabundance of information on ASD had hit the market in direct proportion to the amount of confusion I felt. There was TOO MUCH information. Too many books to buy and digest, and as a parent I didn't have the time, energy or money to buy and read all of them. Plus, most of the information out there was geared toward school and clinical situations, not family life. Sometimes I just wanted someone to boil it down to "Here, try this." What I needed was down-to-earth, easy-to-implement information for daily life situations. "Give me some ideas, let me try them and see if they work," was my plea.

They say that necessity is the mother of invention and sure enough, trial and error over many years with three kids on the spectrum and – ta da – many creative ideas for dealing with daily dilemmas were born out of the chaos. Along the way I also relied on the input of friends who have children like mine who were also struggling, and we shared our ideas with each other. But as we were all on the learning curve together, we all endured many public meltdowns! And in sheer frustration, all of us – kids and parents – endured lots of tears! Many more than might have been necessary if only someone who understood ASD had given us some useful suggestions based on their own knowledge and experience.

Thankfully, you no longer have to work from scratch. Instead, you can lean on the wisdom of others who have gone before you. This book skips right to the immediate, easy-to-flip-to solution that suits the busy lifestyle of families who have a child with ASD. Breaking each topic down into a list of 10 suggestions for commonly faced challenges provides you with a wealth of options, but not so many that you will become overwhelmed by information overload. Try one or more to see which best suits *your* child. If that does the trick, great! If not, go down the list and try others until you find one that works for you. Having this book on hand is like having friends on call when you hit a snag. When you hit a road bump, flip through to the topic heading to see what has worked for your friends. After all, we've been there.

I am familiar with most of the contributors to this book and know that all are hands-on folks in the trenches with their own children and/or have put in years of time with kids and families living with ASD and, therefore, have earned their chops. They understand ASD and they bring a wealth of knowledge and experience to share with us. These aren't random ideas they are throwing out there to see if they stick in order to make a list of 10, but tried-and-true solutions that work for families. I know because I've employed many of their suggestions with my three kids on the spectrum. At the same time, I'm grateful to read new ideas I haven't yet tried and look forward to putting them to good use. It's nice to have some ideas for daily life that I didn't have to figure out all by myself! How wonderful to be able to open a book and instantly put the information to practical use in *real life*.

Top 10 Tips on How to Use This Book

1. Make it your "go-to" book when you hit a bump in the road. Pull it off the shelf as needed and flip to find a multitude of creative suggestions at your fingertips at a moment's notice.

2. Take it on the road: Perfect for a quick flip-through read while waiting for appointments or when you have that rare spare moment anywhere. It beats having to read outdated magazines at the dentist's office!

3. Hide it under the edge of the sofa to pull out for those even rarer uninterrupted moments at home. Try to ignore the ominous silence from the family room where the kids are probably up to mischief. Whatever it is they are doing, you'll feel better about dealing with it after you've taken a break. If you're especially wise, you'll fix yourself a cup of tea while you're reading. The book is well organized, and its easy-to-read format means you can pick it up and then put it down if you hear a loud crash from the family room signaling the end of your peaceful moment.

4. Give it to your extended family members. It's broken into easily digestible bits of information so that they can now feel competent to babysit so you can have some grown-up time with your partner or hubby – or even yourself.

Speaking of husbands, if you are a dad who is reading this, you're a rare gem. My husband didn't crack open *my* book until he was in the hospital and didn't have anything else to read (for the record, he did enjoy it and said, "Ohhhh, is that why we do that?"). My husband appreciates it when we get to the POINT, and this book is excellent at that. No need to make your spouse a list of what to do. Here's one written out for you to share!

Give it to your child's teachers and put the practical at their fingertips, too! Teachers especially like something short and easy-to-peruse because their time is also precious. They appreciate it when we recognize they too have challenges and need practical ideas.

Read aloud and use for topic ideas at parent groups. I've often used lists of topics such as these to bring up discussion points with families. Not only can you share practical tips, the tips will elicit other suggestions from the group as well. Write them down and share with the author because this book is such a great idea I think she needs to write a sequel!

Give a copy to a frazzled and overwhelmed friend or acquaintance. See that mom whose kid is lying on the floor at the grocery store screaming his head off? She'll appreciate receiving this book much more than the stern looks and judgment she gets from *other* people. While sharing ideas, you can lament about how annoying THOSE people are.

Go through it with your child. It was interesting to read through a couple of the lists with my 9-year-old daughter. With surprising insight she was able to point out some of the suggestions that might work best for her. Or, give it to your older child with ASD to read. Say, "You're the expert on ASD, what do you think of this book?" Eventually, we want our kids to self-manage, and reading about practical ideas is a good step in that direction.

DON'T think you have to limit yourself to the items on these lists. Use this book as a way to think about daily dilemmas you face with the child with ASD in your life. When there's a challenge, break it down, ask for suggestions from others and offer your own when people are stressed. Every challenge has a practical solution. You can find one … you might even find 10!

- Kristi Sakai is the author of *Finding Our Way: Practical Solutions for Creating a Supportive Home and Community for the Asperger Syndrome Family*, which was awarded the 2006 Autism Society of America's Literary Work of the Year in the Family/Social Division. Kristi is a national presenter on autism spectrum disorders, pastoral counselor and outspoken advocate for individuals and families. But the greatest passion of her life is being mom to Tom, Kito and Kaede, and wife to Nobuo, all of whom have Asperger Syndrome. She also has a messy house, so please call first before stopping by so she can shovel the toys out of the living room and put the kettle on for tea.

Introduction

Welcome to *Top Ten Tips: A Survival Guide for Families with Children on the Autism Spectrum*. This book is meant to be a quick and helpful tool for navigating your way through everyday activities and occurrences when you live with a child with autism spectrum disorders (ASD).

Several things make this book unique.

1. The book is organized so that you don't have to read through any theories or lengthy descriptions – it is all practical; short and sweet. The stuff you want to know NOW!

2. The book consists of tips contributed by some of the top autism specialists in the world. You get information from the very best – and it is all here in one place.

3. Families who are living with autism every day, just like you, have also contributed tips and suggestions. Many families had to learn these tips the hard way, through trial and error. We are fortunate that they have done the groundwork and that I can share their successes here with you.

4. Throughout the book, you will notice that certain strategies or concepts are marked with an asterisk (*). These are explained in greater detail in the Appendix so they are easier to use.

How to Get the Most out of This Book ... Where You Need It When You Need It

The book is organized so that you can flip to a specific activity or event literally at a moment's notice. For example, if you are looking for tips on haircuts – there are 10 great tips waiting for you. If your child is about to have a birthday party and you are dreading it – there are 10 tips right here to help you out! … And on and on.

Of course, lists of tips are not exhaustive, nor would it be realistic to expect instant solutions to all your everyday challenges. I am sure that you will find some tips that work for you now while others will be better at a later date. Ultimately, some may never be a good fit for your child or family. That's okay. There is still plenty to choose from. The tips are intended to serve as a guide. Some tips may even inspire some creativity on your part. The point is, you don't have to forge the path on your own. You have a survival guide to get you going in the right direction.

A final note, the tips within each topic are not listed in any particular order. Just scan them and start with the one that seems the most promising to you and your family.

Good luck!

Top 10 Positive Things About Having a Child with Autism Spectrum Disorders

My child never lies or deceives. He is truthful and honest. His words are genuine – always.

You will have opportunities to meet people that you never would have met if your child hadn't been diagnosed. Amazing friendships and relationships can be formed around a common bond.

My child follows the rules and wants to do what is right. He aims to please.

My child's heart knows and feels true happiness.

My child's hugs are 100% real and such an honor to receive.

My child gets to be innocent and enjoy his childhood a little longer than others.

My child doesn't understand sarcasm.

My child lives in today. Yesterday is gone, tomorrow's not here yet.

My child's laugh and smile show his pure heart. He has no facades or hidden agendas.

My child teaches me daily to do all of these things again: laugh, play, pretend, listen, be honest and never lie. He teaches me to follow my inner voice and feel with my heart.

Cindy O'Dell

I Can Do It
All by Myself!

Sometimes the most difficult routines for children with autism spectrum disorders are the ones that occur the most frequently, which is all the more reason to get a handle on them.

This chapter provides tips to help with the day-to-day tasks and activities that take place in your home.

Bath and Shower Time

You can use this time for learning (if you aren't too tired). Buy bath tub alphabet toys or shaving cream. Spell words with the letters and stick them to the tub wall. Then show your child how to copy the words into the shaving cream on the bathroom wall. Some kids love baths so you have their undivided attention … and a clean wall afterward.
Joanna Keating-Velasco

My son had problems when he got water put on his head. He didn't like the water running on his face and into his eyes. To get him used to the idea and to help integrate the sensation, I purchased a safety mirror and taped it to the wall of the bathtub. This way he could look at himself as I washed his hair. Being able to see the suds and what was going on lessened his fears and made bath time more fun.
Amy Misencik

Sing a song, like "This is the way we wash our hair, wash our hair, wash our hair …" Your child will learn to associate the song with the activity, and when the song ends, the hair washing ends.
Teresa Cardon

Let your child use shaving cream on the shower doors to play with. It's fun, and she is still getting clean. Children also love to clean the water drips off the door with squeegees.
Cindy O'Dell

Install a moveable-head shower. That way the child can control when the water is on her body and where. It's also adds a little fun in the shower.
Cindy O'Dell

Let the shower be a place where the child can perseverate on favorite things and have some alone time. My son uses this time to recite all his scripts. It is his release time and a safe place to do it. I give him a 20-minute countdown to make it easier from him to transition out.
Holly Reycraft

Baths didn't work for us. Holding on to my child tightly like a bear hug in the shower worked much better. He still loves a shower, not a bath.
Becky Bornhoft

Many children don't like getting water in their eyes. Put a foam visor on the child's head to divert the water as your rinse off his hair. You can also let him hold a washcloth over his eyes to keep the rush of water off.
Teresa Cardon

Foam and plastic books are great distracters in the tub if your child finds books motivating. Other toys can serve the same purpose as long as they are water-friendly. The key is to give your child something else to focus on during bath time.
Teresa Cardon

Create a routine and stick to it! Make a visual support to show the child the steps of the bath: get in, get wet, wash hair, wash body, rinse off, get out, prize/treat. Your child can even use water-friendly crayons to check off each activity once completed. This helps her "see" the process.
Teresa Cardon

Eating

1 When your child stuffs too much food in his mouth at a time, try using an ice cube tray with a forkful of food in each section. This will naturally slow down the process. In addition, have a line drawing of a place to put down the fork with each mouthful. Over time, get rid of the ice cube tray and move to a plate with sections.
Mindy Small

2 Make food fun – paint with carrots, stamp with potatoes, glue macaroni onto paper plates, etc.
Teresa Cardon

3 When introducing a new food, place it on your child's plate for a few days without the expectation that she will eat it. Over time, tolerance to seeing/smelling it will increase, and usually the child will slowly move towards tasting it.
Mindy Small

4 Dips and more dips – don't be afraid to use ketchup, ranch, mustard – whatever makes food more appealing!
Teresa Cardon

When trying to get a child to eat an item he doesn't like, use a First/Then card* and put the undesirable item on top of the FIRST side and the favorite food item on top of the THEN card. It doesn't always work, and that's okay. Sometimes just the fact that the child can sit in front of the undesirable food item is progress. Depending on the student, sometimes just touching the undesirable food to his mouth counts for a reward.
Joanna Keating-Velasco

Breakfast foods aren't only for breakfast anymore! Try scrambled eggs or waffles for dinner. Pizza for breakfast, anyone? Remember, it is about nutrition not tradition.
Teresa Cardon

If your child eats only a limited repertoire of foods of one texture, slowly begin to introduce more foods of the same texture category as opposed to an entirely new texture. From there begin slowly adding very small bits of a new texture.
Mindy Small

Create menus with picture choices to help your child see what the options are. Children feel more in control when they get to make choices.
Teresa Cardon

Put food your child is unsure of on the table near the child, but not on her plate. Help her get used to the idea of the new food by moving it closer and closer until it eventually sits next to her plate.
Teresa Cardon

Have a plastic bin in your pantry or refrigerator full of "O.K." foods for breakfast. Let your child choose. Anything from there will be O.K. The child will feel empowered because he got to choose.
Cindy O'Dell

Teeth Brushing

1 Create a routine that is just for teeth brushing time. Pictures that show each step of the routine take the mystery out of the process. The consistency will help the child understand the steps in the routine and make the process more manageable.
Teresa Cardon

2 Use a light-up toothbrush. While the lights are on, the child keeps brushing, and when the lights go off, she stops. Keep the same routine every day.
Holly Reycraft

3 Find a song, or make up your own, that is reserved for the teeth brushing routine. Sing it every time you brush your child's teeth, or sing it every time the child brushes his own teeth. This also helps children know how long they should brush.
Teresa Cardon

4 Learn how to imitate voices from your child's favorite shows. For example, Elmo and Blues Clues may be able to get your child interested in teeth brushing better than you.
Jamie Blunt

5 Let your child pick out a special toothbrush. Some brushes sing, some vibrate, some feature favorite characters. Motivation to use the brush can go a long way in encouraging your child to actually brush.
Teresa Cardon

Use a visual clock or Time Timer (see Appendix) to show the child exactly how long she needs to brush. The clock displays a red area, and as time passes the red area disappears. When all the red is gone, tooth brushing is finished.
Mindy Small

Tooth brushing does not always have to happen in the bathroom. If your child does better brushing his teeth while standing in front of the television, by all means allow him to brush in front of the television. The final outcome is the same – clean teeth!
Teresa Cardon

Use a First/Then board* to show your child what is going to happen. Let the child brush first, and then you brush. A little bit of control goes a long way.
Teresa Cardon

Get a small mirror and let your child play detective. Have her search for all the cavity bugs and when you "find" one, brush it away.
Teresa Cardon

Get stories about teeth brushing or create your own. Take pictures of all your family members, friends, neighbors, favorite TV characters, etc., brushing their teeth. Read the story together at various times throughout the day and definitely read it once before it is time to brush teeth. Refer to the various elements in the story while your child is brushing her teeth. The story can take the power struggle away from you *and* make it more motivating.
Teresa Cardon

Potty Training

1 Place a visual target in the toilet water to show a boy where to aim. Try cheerios or fruit loops; they flush easily.
Mindy Small

2 Get a doll that pees. Have the doll pee on the potty. Encourage the doll – act as though it were real. Give all the attention to the doll, including giving the doll the reinforcer (skittles, M&M's, whatever works for your child). This provides a model for the child, who can then understand the reward ahead of time.
Cindy O'Dell

3 If your child resists sitting on the toilet without a diaper, begin by cutting a small hole in the diaper and having the child sit. As the child becomes more tolerant, increase the size of the diaper opening until the diaper can be removed without the child resisting.
Mindy Small

4 To show a boy where to stand to urinate, cut out large footprints that depict where to place his feet in front of the toilet.
Mindy Small

5 When teaching the child to use a public restroom, cover the automatic toilet sensor while the child holds her hands over her ears. The unexpected flush and the loud noise can be overwhelming.
Jenny Clark Brack

Create a reward chart* with stickers or smiley faces so that your child can see just how much fun going potty can be. Rewards can vary depending on the type of activity that was happening in the bathroom (i.e., pooping vs. peeing).
Teresa Cardon

Just sitting on the potty must be a positive experience, so reward your child even if she does not go to the bathroom but sits and tries.
Teresa Cardon

Let your child engage in fun activities while sitting on the potty. Shaving cream, books or even videos can encourage him to relax and get the job done.
Teresa Cardon

Make sure your child experiences what it feels like to be wet or messy. Some diapers and pull-ups are so good that the child may not be uncomfortable when he pees or poops. As messy as it sounds, old-fashioned underwear may still be the best bet. Also, going back to diapers is not a good plan. Many children wait until they leave the house to go to the bathroom because they have learned that mom and dad will put a diaper on them.
Teresa Cardon

Have a potty party. Plan several days to stay at home. Make sure your child drinks lots of fluids and has easy access to a potty (limited clothes, prime location). Then be consistent. Set the child on the potty every 30 minutes without fail. Keep the child in underwear so she can feel the wetness when she does make a mistake. Do not leave the house and put pull-ups on your child, particularly when she is first learning. If your child is truly ready to be potty trained, going back to diapers will be confusing.
Teresa Cardon

Cleaning up Room

1 Label drawers in the child's bedroom to indicate what belongs in each drawer. This facilitates independent participation in clean-up, specifically putting away laundry and personal belongings. Be sure to label each drawer in a way your child understands (written word, photograph, line drawing, etc.).
Mindy Small

2 Let the child select a hamper to keep in his room. Make a big deal out of him being old enough to have his own hamper and then create a point board for every article of dirty clothing thrown in. After an appropriate number of points, give a small reward. Depending on the child, the reward may be given twice a day or once a week. Later this chore may be expanded to putting the clothes into the laundry room or simply putting them into the basket ready for transport.
Joanna Keating-Velasco

3 Allow the child to pick out an inexpensive light-weight upright vacuum at the store or in a magazine. Initially using hand-over-hand, if necessary, have him be responsible for vacuuming a small area for a check mark on a chart. Once his room is vacuumed, he earns a small reward. If the noise bothers the child, let him wear headphones and listen to music.
Joanna Keating-Velasco

4 Children can put away toys if they know where everything goes. Put pictures on walls above the area where big toys go and pictures on shelves where small toys are stored. Be sure to teach the child how to be successful by helping her through the process several times.
Teresa Cardon

5 Use plastic bins with pictures on the outside to help organize toys with lots of small parts like Legos and blocks. This also cuts down the frustration of mixing pieces of different toys together.
Teresa Cardon

6 Use a basket for large stuffed animals as a quick cleaning solution. Children can throw the stuffed animals in the basket – and the job is done.
Teresa Cardon

7 A clear, physical structure is vital when children are learning how to care for their own space. Strategically place furniture in the room so that each area has a distinct function. For example, a book shelf to mark off a quiet area or a rug to identify the train and car area. You'll be surprised at the positive results.
Teresa Cardon

8 Break the cleaning process down into small, more manageable chunks. Create one task that has to be done four or five days a week as opposed to cleaning the whole room in one day, which can be overwhelming. Create a chart to keep track of tasks. For example,
Monday = clean up books
Tuesday = clean up toys
Wednesday = vacuum floor
Thursday = put clothes away, etc.
Teresa Cardon

Create a cleaning ladder (a visual reward system) so your child can see each step that gets her closer to a motivating treat or toy at the top rung. On each rung of the ladder, list something that needs to be cleaned in her room. Every time the child cleans something, she "climbs" a rung and gets to move the picture of the treat/toy to the next step (Velcro works great for this).
Teresa Cardon

Try photographs, like an "I Spy" book. Clean the child's room and then take photos of each area – bed, book-shelves, closet, open floor space, wall hooks – and put them into a book, very short and precise, about 10 pages. Read the book together in the child's room each morning. As you read each page, do an "I Spy" of the given area look-ing for things that are out of place. The child can either put them into place immediately and come back for the rest of the book or wait until the end of the book.
Kathryn Jolley

Getting Ready in the Morning

1 Use a mini visual schedule* to depict each step along the way. For example, brush teeth, wash face, get dressed, eat breakfast, use bathroom, and wait for bus. Be sure to create the schedule in a form your child understands (written words, objects, photos, etc.). This can also be referred to as a "to do" list and, if it helps, items can be checked off as they are completed.
Mindy Small

2 Teach your child to wake up to an alarm clock. It is common for parents to wake their children for school. However, as your child grows older, it's a good idea to teach him to wake up to an alarm clock. You may have to experiment with buzzers, music, and various degrees of volume. For individuals who are particularly hard to wake, it helps to have them walk across the room to turn off the alarm clock. Eventually, this skill would include the child learning to set the alarm clock. A more advanced skill would involve the child being able to estimate the amount of time needed to get ready and determine what time the alarm should be set for.
Diane Adreon

3 Teach your child to learn to use visual cues to remember tasks. This might involve keeping medicine in a certain place, so he remembers to take it at breakfast each morning or writing lunch on a piece of paper and taping it onto the school backpack to remember to bring lunch.
Diane Adreon

4 Try teaching your child to tie his shoes by using a real shoe and shoelaces of two different colors for practice. Once he gets that, transition to his own shoes with same-color laces.
Renata Irving

5 Lay out the child's clothes on the floor just like they would look when put on. Another option is to stack the items on top of each other in the order that your child needs to put them on: underwear, shorts, t-shirt, socks, and shoes.
Cindy O'Dell

6 Use a soft hairbrush and count to 10. If your child still can't tolerate the brush, put some squirt gel in your hand and use your hand to fix her hair.
Holly Reycraft

7 Help your child establish healthy routines: shower or bathe every 24 hours, comb and brush hair, put on deodorant, wear clean clothes, etc. Many children find it easier (in the long run) to follow rules such as taking a shower or bath every day, rather than every two to three days. Teach your child each step in washing properly (e.g., four times across each armpit with a soapy washcloth). Poor hygiene is not tolerated well by the community.
Diane Adreon

8 If the child has trouble dressing, it can help to create a chart for her that pertains to her special interest – Disney princesses, for example. Each day that she gets dressed without a major tantrum, she receives a princess sticker. When she has accumulated five stickers, she is rewarded with a Disney princess doll. With each five-sticker success, increase expectations for her behavior until she is able to dress without the slightest hint of a tantrum. This needs to be adjusted based on age and function. For example, a younger child may need a reward after just one sticker. Also, as it becomes easier for the child to regulate her behavior with regard to dressing, you can decrease the significance of the reward (e.g., a princess coloring book instead of a doll) until none is needed.
Jennifer Frandsen

9 Put a hanging shoe holder in the closet and use it to organize each outfit for the week. There are usually five slots, and each slot can hold a pair of underwear, pants, shirt, socks and shoes – one complete outfit. When everything is together in one place, it provides clarity and structure.
Teresa Cardon

10 Get backpacks ready the night before, and be sure that your child is part of the process. Even if the child is only putting one thing in the backpack, she is still learning to plan ahead and taking responsibility. Create a checklist for the child to use when she is ready for more responsibility.
Teresa Cardon

CHAPTER 2

Trarel Time

Traveling together as a family should be a part of every child's life. It is not always easy to travel with a child who has an autism spectrum disorder, because the disruption in routine can be significant and upset him and everybody else around him. This chapter provides tips and ideas that not only make family travel possible but fun, too!

Traveling

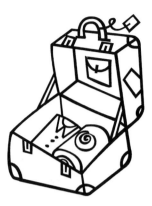

1 Ask locals about the best places to visit. You might find some great out-of-the way and quiet locations that your family can investigate together. It's not where you go that matters. Kids remember what you all do together, not the destination.
Joanna Keating-Velasco

2 Go online to autism blogs* (personal websites maintained as a discussion forum) and get suggestions of great places to take kids with similar needs and challenges. There are many autism blogs on the Internet that offer support, products, and information.
Joanna Keating-Velasco

3 Camp in your backyard. Pop up a tent and grab the sleeping bags. There is no risk, because if it doesn't work out, you walk back into the house and crawl into bed. If it does work out, next time try a local campground. Then continue to expand out farther, if it's a good experience.
Joanna Keating-Velasco

4 If your child becomes anxious when it comes to traveling, get a backpack for her to carry her favorite things in. That way she will always have access to her special things, which is particularly important during stressful moments.
Jamie Blunt

5 Create a picture check-off list of all the items you need for long trips. Make sure to include some blanks for the child to add items that you didn't think of (like teddy bear, favorite game or puzzle). You may need to put a number next to the item if you

need several items (like underwear, shirts, etc.). If the child is able to match up the items himself, let him. If the child needs help, perhaps you grab the item and then let him check it off the list with a marker. This way he is part of the process, so if something is forgotten, you can mention the list.
Joanna Keating-Velasco

Keep a toiletry bag packed and ready to go so you don't have to mess with your home supplies. That way you won't forget anything either.
Joanna Keating-Velasco

PLAN AHEAD!!! Use a weekly or monthly calendar to show your child when the trip will happen.
Mindy Small

Toilet paper countdown – hang the exact number of toilet paper squares that show how many more days until you go on vacation, return from vacation, or a parent will return from a business trip. At the same time each day, one piece is ripped off and thrown away.
Mindy Small

When possible, use photographs or brochures to help prepare your child for what the travel destination will look like.
Mindy Small

Practice hiking or beachcombing by creating a nature guidebook. Buy a small photo book at the dollar store. On each page put a little picture or Internet image of an item (rock, flower, bee, bird, snake, tree, bush, waterfall, etc.) that you might encounter on your hike. When your child or you notice the items, take a digital photo, which can later be added to the photo album. It will make the hike more interesting and create a souvenir.
Joanna Keating-Velasco

Airplane Rides

1. Create a fake "passport" (make it look somewhat real) to help your child keep track of the various steps you go through at the airport. List typical travel experiences, such as baggage claim, ticket counter, flight attendant, pilot, shuttle driver, taxi driver, hotel, front desk clerk, etc., and have the child hand the passport to various people along the way while you explain he is getting his passport "stamped." Ask the person your child is "checking in with" to sign the passport, or even stamp it if there is a stamp nearby. The passport makes a fun souvenir, too.
Joanna Keating-Velasco

2. Wrap up 10 items (books, word search games, toys, sensory gadgets, etc.) in several layers of wrapping paper. Every so often on the plane, hand the child a present to open. The toys don't have to be new. The novelty of a toy being wrapped makes it interesting. The unwrapping takes time off the plane trip, and the recently opened toy becomes a novel activity (at least for a moment!).
Joanna Keating-Velasco

3. Create a personal story for your child to read that will tell him ahead of time what he can expect at the airport. If possible, include pictures. Be sure to include parking, security, baggage claim, the airplane seats, bathroom, and who will be meeting you at the other end. Read it often before your trip and take it with you for the child to refer to during the trip.
Cindy O'Dell

4 While on an airplane, bringing along video games like a Nintendo or a portable Playstation can save your life.
Holly Reycraft

5 For children who use visual forms of communication, create a choice board* for use with the flight attendant so your child can interact and request his choice of drink and/or snack.
Mindy Small

6 Bathrooms are loud and bouncy on airplanes. Go to the bathroom with your child and wait to flush until he has left. Also, make sure you go to the bathroom on the plane right before descent. The flight attendants are serious when they say that everyone must remain in their seats at the end of the flight.
Cindy O'Dell

7 For higher functioning children, write a list of 20 items that you see in the airline sales magazine (e.g., map of destination airport in the back, ad for a certain restaurant). Challenge the child to find them as fast as she can.
Joanna Keating-Velasco

8 Borrow or bring a DVD player (charged up!!) and allow the child to watch one movie on the plane. Be prepared for the battery to die. Have a backup plan.
Joanna Keating-Velasco

9 Bring Colorforms™ or other vinyl stickers. They stick to the windows and can provide lots of quiet entertainment on a long flight.
Teresa Cardon

10 Have your child decorate his suitcase before the trip. Watching for his unique decorations gives him something to look forward to while waiting for the luggage to come off the plane. It also acts as the reward for waiting when he sees his special bag coming.
Cindy O'Dell

Hotel Rooms

1 Bring your child's blanket and pillow from home. It's always more comfortable having your own stuff at a hotel.
Joanna Keating-Velasco

2 Get a hotel room on the first floor. Let the kids jump on the bed! Set a timer if you need to limit the activity.
Joanna Keating-Velasco

3 If your child likes to swim, call the hotel ahead of time to make sure there is a pool and that it is open.
Joanna Keating-Velasco

4 Ask the hotel desk clerk or concierge what local things a child might like that aren't necessarily commercial. Sometimes the easy local tips are the best (versus the amusement park). For example, there may be a swimming pool with a waterslide that your child will enjoy just as much, or maybe even more, as spending all day at a huge water park.
Joanna Keating-Velasco

5 Before you go to a hotel, let your child sleep on an air mattress for several nights as a special treat. Then when you go to the hotel, bring the air mattress, a pump, sheets and pillows from home. Your child will get to sleep in a bed she is already familiar with.
Amy Misencik

Don't hesitate to make changes to a hotel room to accommodate your child's needs and/or interests (move a bed, temporar-
ily hang a photo on the wall, etc.).
Mindy Small

Bring your own safety devices such as outlet plugs, window
locks, toilet latches, etc. Even in close quarters, your child can get
into dangerous situations quickly.
Teresa Cardon

Use pictures to create a story about the things that will happen
when you stay at a hotel. This can help make things feel familiar when you arrive. Go to the hotel's website for pictures, etc.
Sometimes, you can also take a virtual tour online and view the
hotel ahead of time.
Teresa Cardon

If your child is a quick mover, be sure you find a hotel where the
door opens into an indoor as opposed to an outdoor hallway.
Teresa Cardon

Hang bells on the hotel door that leads to the hallway so that
you will hear it open and close any time, day or night.
Teresa Cardon

Trips to Relatives

1 Compile a photo book of relatives you are going to see. Keep it with you and look at it often. Talk to your child about the book and each person in it. Include pictures of their house, car, pets, where your child will sleep. You want as few surprises as possible when you arrive.
Cindy O'Dell

2 Take pictures of all your child's favorite things at home so she will have a little book of favorites that she can look at during the trip. Being able to see things from home provides some comforting downtime.
Cindy O'Dell

3 Pack food that your child can eat. There may not be any food at the relatives' that he will eat. Share about special diets or food preferences to help the relatives understand and not be offended that you brought your own food.
Cindy O'Dell

4 Plan for some activities ahead of time, if possible. Decide on several special activities and then create a calendar so that your child has something special to look forward to each day of the trip.
Teresa Cardon

5 Bring your child's favorite blanket, pillow, toy, etc., so she has something of her very own in a strange new place.
Teresa Cardon

Share plenty of information with your relatives ahead of time so they are not caught off guard by special diet and safety needs, behaviors, routines, etc., when you arrive. They do not know what it is like to live with your child, and such advance notice can help create a positive experience for everyone.
Teresa Cardon

Practice and role play with your child ahead of time what it will be like to stay at someone else's house. Discuss the rules for eating at a different house, how to say no thanks when the child doesn't want something that's being offered, what rooms he can go into and what rooms are out of bounds, rules for not going through other people's drawers or cabinets, etc. Don't assume that your child knows the rules. Lay them out clearly and deliberately.
Teresa Cardon

If possible, try to have a room or space at your relative's house that is for your family and child to use as a home base. If your child needs time away from the chaos and noise that often accompany large family gatherings, it is nice to have a space to retreat to – all for you.
Teresa Cardon

Even though you may not be able to keep the same daily routine that you do at home, try to establish a routine at the relatives'. Decide on a schedule of outings, meals, downtime, video watching, etc. Create a way to share it with your child, through pictures or written words, and then stick to it as best you can. Some routine is better than none.
Teresa Cardon

People change a lot, even over short lengths of time (new hair color, different haircut). Ask relatives whom you haven't seen for a while to send a recent photo ahead of time. You can even ask them to take a picture of their car and house. Looking at the pictures helps create a sense of comfort for the child.
Cindy O'Dell

Long Car Trips

1 Download from the Net navigational directions from your point of departure to arrival. That way your child can follow not only the written instructions but also the visual map and be the navigator.
Josie Santomauro

2 When preparing your child for a long car ride, create a clear plan, similar to a visual schedule*, to indicate how long he will have to sit in the car, what he can do while waiting in the car, what he can't do while in the car, what he is going to do when he gets out of the car, etc.
Teresa Cardon

3 Use visual task lists. You can include particular places of interest you will pass on the way in a check-off format.
Kari Dunn Buron

4 To give a sense of time/distance, use the mileage to your child's school and multiply it by how far you are expecting to travel. Let your child see the map and the mileage chart, and then prompt her to check off every 5-10 miles, depending on how far the school ride is.
Kari Dunn Buron

Create a 5-point scale* for voice volume (if this is a problem in your family). Review the scale with your child prior to the trip. If his voice volume gets too high, you can prompt him with a number ("bring it down to a 3," or "it's late, time for 2 voices"). *Kari Dunn Buron*

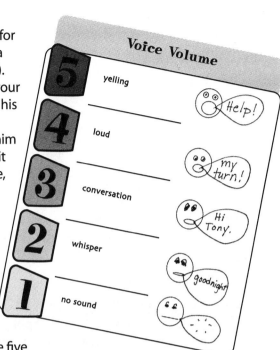

A great little system for communicating the passage of time in the car is "Five Stars." Explain verbally or in a story that your drive will take five stars. Give the child a cardboard strip with five pieces of Velcro on it and a picture or symbol of where you are going at the end of the Velcro dots. Make five stars, each with a piece of Velcro on the back. At various points during the ride, put a star on the strip and say, for example, "Four more stars, then we are at grandma's house." This system can be used over and over again for different trips because you are in control of how quickly or slowly you put on the stars. You may want to practice this system using shorter distances prior to a big trip. It works for airplane trips as well.
Kari Dunn Buron

Let your child take his favorite CDs, DVDs and books on the trip. With the help of a portable DVD player, time can fly.
Amy Bixler Coffin

Look for something to count like animals or cars. Make a list of how many you see. Take photos or color pictures of the items you are searching for and then make a scrapbook to remember the trip later.
Becky Bornhoft

Stop often for movement breaks. Let your child know how long until a movement break is coming. Visual supports work well. For example, create a sticker chart you can add stickers to every five minutes. When you get six stickers on the chart, it is time for a movement break. Or use a timer. Just be sure your child knows how it works so he can see how long it is until a break is coming. Have fun and favorite activities available during the movement break.
Teresa Cardon

Create a list of things your child can look for along the way, red cars, green signs, motor homes, cars pulling boats, etc. Laminate the sheet and have the child mark down every time she sees an item. It helps pass the time and places the focus on something other than the ride itself.
Teresa Cardon

Disneyland/ Disney World Theme Parks

1 Before leaving for a trip to Disneyland or the Magic Kingdom, obtain a written note from your child's medical provider on a prescription pad to include the child's diagnosis and how the diagnosis will impede her ability to access and enjoy the park(s). Here is an example:

To whom it may concern:
My patient (child's name) has been diagnosed with Asperger Syndrome, which is on the autism spectrum. It would be extremely difficult for her to wait in lines. Your understanding with this matter would be tremendously appreciated.
Signature, M.D.

This note will allow you to obtain a Guest Assistance Card for everyone in your party, up to six people. The pass allows access to rides and attractions without having to wait in what can be more than hour-long lines. This won't make you "stand out" because Disney offers a new option called "fast pass," which limited members of the general public can access at certain times of the day, so you just stand with them.
Michele Walker

When visiting amusement parks, try to go on a weekday during off-peak times. Call the park ahead of time and explain that you have a child with special needs and want to visit during the least crowded time. They will help you make plans.
Teresa Cardon

The walk from the parking lot to the park entrance can be long and exhausting. Often there are special trams to transport guests, but if possible, have another driver park the car and drop you and your child off at the entrance. You don't want your child to get nervous about the tram ride or the huge parking structure before the day at the amusement park even gets started.
Teresa Cardon

A Guest Assistance Card does not work in the food arena. The lines for food can be over an hour long. Bring your own food or eat lunch at 11 a.m. before the crowds hit. Bring something to drink.
Michele Walker

Get several maps of the theme park ahead of time. Use them to make picture cards for visuals. You can map out your day, and the child will know what to expect.
Joanna Keating-Velasco

Read books about Disneyworld (*Walt Disney World & Orlando for Dummies 2008* and *Birbaum's Walt Disney World 2008*). These books give you an accurate idea of what you can expect on the rides and attractions. You may want to measure your child so you can rule out beforehand attractions for which he does not meet the height requirement. Go on line and search for images of Disney attractions and expose your child to the visuals to get an idea of his comfort level. A lot of rides take place in the dark, for example.
Michele Walker

Go online to www.mouseplanet.com and research what months and days at Disneyland have the fewest guests. Then arrive at the parking lot 45 minutes prior to the gates opening. This way you can be at the front gate and get into Main Street just in time for the park to open. Use the restroom. Then get a Fast Pass for one of the big rides to use later. Enjoy a relatively calm morning. Seek out great rides with no lines. Visit characters.
Joanna Keating-Velasco

Consider getting a stroller. Even if your child is older, he may appreciate the stroller after a while. If nothing else, the stroller is a great place to put your stuff.
Michele Walker

If you have more than one child, you can utilize CHILD SWAP. One adult must wait in line with one child. When you get to an employee, ask for a CHILD SWAP pass. This means that an adult not waiting in line can walk around with the child who has trouble waiting. When the first child and adult finish the ride, they transfer the CHILD SWAP pass to the adult and child who were walking around, who can now go right through with no wait.
Joanna Keating-Velasco

If it's the child's birthday, go immediately to City Hall and notify them. The child will get to hear a special Disney character on the town hall phone. The child also gets a special sticker and is recognized by name all day long.
Joanna Keating-Velasco

CHAPTER 3

Friendship Factors

lay and social interactions are important elements of childhood. Children on the spectrum often need supports to make play and other social interactions successful and enjoyable. The tips in this chapter can help turn play dates and social interactions into positive experiences for all.

Play with Peers and Siblings

1. Observe what your child does naturally during free play with peers. This will help in identifying realistic and meaningful play activities at your child's developmental level while also acknowledging his interaction style and play preferences.
Pamela Wolfberg

2. Create natural opportunities for your child to play with a few select children on a regular and consistent basis. If possible, choose socially competent peers who are compatible with your child and have similar play interests.
Pamela Wolfberg

3. Because children with ASD often respond well to structure/routine/schedules, put playing with siblings on your child's schedule for a specified time with a pleasurable activity or treat to follow. For example, playtime is at 3:00; at 4:00 sit down to eat cookies and watch a TV show together. In this way play time simply becomes part of their routine. It helps if rules are posted in writing and/or pictures.
Kristi Sakai

4. Set up the play environment so that it is restricted to a reasonable amount of space, clearly defined by boundaries (furniture, shelves, etc.), and explicitly organized play materials (farm animals and farm, race track and cars, etc.).
Pamela Wolfberg

5. Structure the play session with a clear beginning, middle, and end. For example, you can verbally tell the children, or show them with

pictures: *First* we are going to play with the cars, *next* we are going to jump on the trampoline, and *last* we are going to have a snack.
Pamela Wolfberg

Structure play activities that incorporate activity routines and visual supports. For example, create a visual support that describes the steps needed to play grocery check-out. Each child can also wear a visual support that states their role in the activity, such as a ball cap that says "Check-Out" or an apron that says "Bakery Department."
Pamela Wolfberg

Center the play session around play materials, activities, and themes that require social interaction and are motivating for your child as well as the other children. For example, arts and crafts are great ways to create social interactions between groups of children and are highly motivating at the same time.
Pamela Wolfberg

Guide the children to play effectively by monitoring initiations, providing support (but only as needed), and facilitating social communication and play exchanges geared to each child's unique interests, ability, and experience. For example, when a child is playing a favorite board game with other children, teach the other children how to provide an appropriate model each time they take their turn.
Pamela Wolfberg

Create cooperative arrangements where the children have to work together to be successful. Give one child the farm animals and the other child the farmhouse or give one child the pieces to the game and the other child the game board. Be sure to facilitate success the first few times and then back out so the children can negotiate on their own.
Teresa Cardon

Create turn-taking supports to help the typical child and the child with ASD know when it is time to take their turn. Photographs of each person on a 3x5 card work great. Just turn the card over when it is the other person's turn to play a video game, ride on the swing, etc.
Teresa Cardon

Play Dates

1 Make your house an exciting place to visit so that typical peers are motivated to come often; for example, by having the latest videogame system. Be sure to have fun snacks on hand and keep visits structured and organized so that no one gets frustrated, and everyone has a good time.
Cindy O'Dell

2 Begin by using toys/games that are of high interest to your child with ASD. Use a turn-taking card* with photos of all children playing so it is visually clear to your child when they can have a turn and when they must wait.
Mindy Small

3 Provide the peer with something the child with ASD must have in order to participate. For example, give the peer the only glue bottle during an art activity so there will be a need for interaction between them.
Mindy Small

4 Make available highly motivating play materials, themes, and pop-culture activities to promote successful social interactions between children on the autism spectrum and their peers and siblings.
Heather McCracken

5 Set up regular times for children to play and socialize in a highly structured yet naturalistic environment. Find consistent peers to include in play and give them a clear job to do during the play

time. Books are available (see Appendix) to help you design peer programs for your child.
Heather McCracken

Get out of the way! Provide adult support but move out of the social interactions as soon as possible. You are not the child's peer!
Heather McCracken

Choose the right friends. Children who are patient and willing to have a grown-up intervene when necessary are ideal play dates. Children who have a lot of energy and tend to run around the house without any interest in engaging your child are not good matches and can create a frustrating experience for everyone.
Teresa Cardon

Create a visual schedule* for the play date, and try to include play time, snack time, outside time, and some downtime. A little bit of structure can go a long way in providing a positive play experience.
Teresa Cardon

Keep it short. Play dates do not have to be all-day events. Start out slowly, particularly if it is with a new child, so you can see how it goes. Thirty minutes may be plenty the first time. You can build from there.
Teresa Cardon

Play dates are not a time for you to plan to be involved exten-sively with another activity. While you don't want to hover, you must be able to step in when needed. The goal is for your child to have successful social interactions with a peer, and sometimes that means a grown-up needs to step in.
Teresa Cardon

Board Games: Playing, Winning and Losing

1 *Candy Land* is a great game for young and old alike. It is basic and teaches color matching and turn taking, besides winning and losing. And it's fun!
Joanna Keating-Velasco

2 Lose a game on purpose and act like a sore loser to let your child see what it looks like. Debrief later and discuss what would have been a better way to behave.
Joan Clark

3 Play the *Lose to Win!* game. Set up a grid with anywhere from 5 to 25 squares. Every time your child loses and maintains his cool, mark off a square and make a big deal about it. When the grid is filled, it's reward time for your child, who is learning how to lose with grace – a winning attitude for sure!
Joan Clark

4 Pretend you don't know, and let your child offer guidance on how to play the game, whose turn it is, etc. Modeling and being a "kid" again helps, too.
Cindy O'Dell

Teach your child that she doesn't always win. Use personalized stories* and role playing to prepare her. Then she won't mind as much if the other player wins.
Cindy O'Dell

Have the child help set up and take apart the game. There is a lot of fun and interaction time in setting up the game, especially if it's a new game. It is a great time to work on following directions and teamwork.
Cindy O'Dell

After Christmas is a great time to get good deals on games that are on clearance sale. Stock up. The out-of-the-ordinary games sometimes turn out to be the best.
Cindy O'Dell

Throw out the rules of the game and make up others that work better for your kids. As long as they are interacting and having fun, you have accomplished your goal.
Cindy O'Dell

Show your child video models of good losers. Sporting events always have examples of losers (be sure to choose the positive examples!). Also, you can take video of family members, friends, classmates, etc., playing games and demonstrating good losing skills.
Teresa Cardon

If winning and losing is a tough concept for your child to grasp, have "prizes" for both the winner and the loser. That way both can look forward to something after the game is over. Slowly work up to helping the child lose gracefully. The child can get smaller and smaller "prizes" interspersed with verbal praise until eventually he is able to lose the game without receiving a tangible prize.
Cindy O'Dell

After-School Clubs and Extracurricular Activities

1 Don't be afraid to try new after-school activities. Just because playing on the soccer team didn't work out doesn't mean a bowling team will also be a disaster. You never know when you might find your child's niche.
Wallis A. Simpson

2 Create a club at school based on your child's special interest: maps, airplanes, animals, video games, horses, etc. There are often other kids who find the same types of topics interesting. Make sure the group is motivating and fun for everyone. Including food is usually a good way to attract kids.
Teresa Cardon

3 Get a school staff member to be your campus support in creating an after-school program that focuses on the child's strengths and incorporates peer interactions. Focus on the child's academic strengths or interests and then create an enrichment class that targets that area (art masterpiece [www.teachartathome.com], puzzle partners [www.educationworld.com/a_lesson/dailylp/dailylp004.shtml], ooey gooey science [www.ooeygooey.com], etc.).
Teresa Cardon

4 Work with the staff at your child's school to create a Circle of Friends* group for your child. Bring in materials about different programs and decide as a team what type of program will work best for the school. When school staff know you are willing to be a part of the process, they aren't as intimidated at getting things started.
Teresa Cardon

5 Girl Scouts and Boy Scouts can be great places for working on peer interactions. Both organizations support friendship and acceptance, and the right group can be a safe place to work on social interactions. Be sure that you prepare the leaders* and group members to support your child by sharing information that is important for your child to be successful.
Teresa Cardon

6 Consider a gymnastics program that offers classes for children on the spectrum. The sensory input they receive from many of the activities is very regulating; that is, they bring about balance to their sensory system. Be sure the coaches are experienced and caring. It is also important to find a small class size and good student-coach ratios.
Teresa Cardon

7 Create an introductory letter* for Scout leaders, coaches, and other facilitators ahead of time to share information about your child. You can also create handouts for all the parents and children to educate them about your child's strengths and needs.
Michelle Pomeroy

8 Contact local special needs groups to find out if there are any special leagues (baseball, soccer, or basketball) in your area. Get involved on a team. Accept "baby steps" of enthusiasm if your child is not excited at first. For the first practice, perhaps just arriving and seeing the building is okay. The next time, the child watches 20 minutes of a practice. The third time, she participates with you for 5 minutes. This may never be something your child wants to get involved with, but give it a season of at least trying to allow the child to really see if she is interested.
Joanna Keating-Velasco

Local zoos, aquariums, libraries, etc., offer great programs. Check out the event ahead of time to determine if it is a good fit for your child. Pick programs that are small in terms of the number of children and high on structure. Then contact the organization and let them know that you are planning to enroll your child and that this will be a unique opportunity for them to educate other youth in the community about autism.
Teresa Cardon

If your child is not ready for large groups, start by trading an afternoon with a neighborhood mom. Find a mom who is will-ing to put together two or three organized activities that both of your children can participate in (you may need to provide some extra support here –you want the other mom to feel successful). You can trade homes every other week to help your child get used to an after-school routine that involves other people and places.
Teresa Cardon

CHAPTER 4

Family
Ins and Outs

Being part of a family means taking part in family routines and activities. It is important to plan for ways that a child with autism can be included in family dynamics. This chapter provides tips to assist families in creating effective ways to understand and include the child with autism spectrum disorders. Important life skills are learned along the way.

Informing Relatives About Autism Spectrum Disorders

1 The child with ASD needs the whole family on board. Relatives want to understand ASD, so provide a family forum. Make it a fun event. Get a discussion-oriented book about ASD.
Joanna Keating-Velasco

2 Finding the right resources helps a lot. The *Five for Fighting* video (www.whatkindofworlddoyouwant.com/videos/%20view/ id/408214) is a great way to share information about autism. (See the Appendix for other ideas.)
Becky Bornhoft

3 Find videos and/or information packets for your family to read. Resources* that can cover all the hard-to-answer questions are great when you may not be ready to explain specifics to everybody. Give relatives the videos and books you want them to read. Don't wait for them to search for answers on their own.
Cindy O'Dell

4 Use the poem "10 Things Every Child with Autism Wishes You Knew" by Ellen Notbohm (see Appendix) to share information about your child with family members.
Becky Bornhoft

Be clear with relatives/neighbors/schools about what events or activities you will and will not be able to attend or participate in. Be willing to say no if a given activity is not in your child's best interest. When appropriate, ask relatives and friends to schedule events further apart to allow your child to wind down in between. The earlier you address this with people, especially family members, the more willing they are to help accommodate your needs.
Kathryn Jolley

Go to your family prepared with facts. They may have heard a couple of things about autism in the media or they may have a very limited frame of reference. Your job is to educate them so that they can be a part of the solution and not add to any panic or confusion.
Teresa Cardon

Give your relatives something to do. Relatives often feel a sense of loss and helplessness when learning that a family member has been diagnosed. A book and other resources that give them practical strategies that they can understand and implement right away will help empower them. See the Appendix for ideas.
Teresa Cardon

You know your family best. If it would work better to tell them all in a large group, then plan a gathering. If you think that a few private lunches or get-togethers would be more effective, take that route. There is no perfect answer, and you need to feel comfortable in the setting you choose.
Teresa Cardon

Your family may not know how to react to the word *autism*. They may experience a lot of negative or sad emotions and confusion. Some people go through a grieving process upon learning about the diagnosis. Denial is a common emotion. You can only provide the information and facts about autism. You cannot force anyone to accept it.
Teresa Cardon

Let your family know how much you need them. Now is the time to ask for help. Let them help you.
Teresa Cardon

Siblings

1 Be sure to put aside time for your typical kid(s); this can be fun "alone time," field trips, reading and relaxing, beauty afternoons – anything to make them feel special and worthy of your sole attention. Try to do some of this every day, even if you are exhausted.
Lynne Stern Feiges

2 Consider getting your typical child a therapist of his own if he is having problems. This will not only help the child work through the issues, it will also let him know that he has someone special to turn to, and that it's not just the sibling with ASD who has the whole outside world coming to help.
Lynne Stern Feiges

3 Enlist other adults to give attention to your typical child. This can be a neighbor, another parent, a relative, or all of the above. You can't do it all.
Lynne Stern Feiges

4 Be conscious of fairness. For instance, if the sibling with ASD is getting "forbidden" treats as edible rewards for a given task, give some to the typical child, too. If one gets it, the other should.
Lynne Stern Feiges

5 Implement a structured reward program for the typical child, if age appropriate. This will send the message that the child can work for extras and that there is stability in the house.
Lynne Stern Feiges

Remember that siblings have the right to freely express their emotions even if they are frustrated or angry with the child with ASD as long as the expression is constructive and not destructive.
Josie Santomauro

Allow siblings to read books that talk about autism in a kid-friendly manner. There are many great examples listed in the Appendix.
Teresa Cardon

Let your child's siblings help teach new skills. Sometimes a child will respond better to a sibling than to a parent. Besides, it's a way for the siblings to become involved.
Wallis A. Simpson

Always make sure the siblings have at least one thing that is all their own. Whether it is a sport, Scouts, etc., allow them something they don't have to share or compromise about. Make every effort to make sure they don't miss any scheduled games, activities, etc. You don't miss therapies for your child with ASD. Try to follow the same policy for siblings.
Cindy O'Dell

Remember that one-on-one time with mom and dad is essential, even if it's just a meal at Taco Bell. Park the car and go in. Sit down. Make it a big deal that the sibling is out with just you – talk about school or his or her friends. Go to a movie. Make note not to talk about anything ASD. Make this a time when the sibling exclusively has your eyes, ears, and thoughts.
Cindy O'Dell

When a Parent Is Away

1 Use a monthly calendar with the parent's photo on each day. For the days when the parent will be out of town, place a large red X over the face. This increases visual clarity.
Mindy Small

2 Create a simple photo book detailing items like
- Picture of mom and dad with the words "I love you"
- Picture of caretaker saying "I love you"
- Calendar to mark off the days or hours until the parents return
- Pictures of activities to do while parents are gone
- Picture of where the parents are
- Note from parents
- A recorded message from mom and dad to go with the book

Joanna Keating-Velasco

3 If the parents are going on a major trip, hang up a world map. Then use a picture representing the mode of transport they will be using (plane, bus, car, taxi, or train) to visually show the places the parents are visiting. Depending on the child's ability, use one transport visual moving along the map or use stickers and keep the visual moving "on a track" to show progress. Have a simple calendar next to the map with a start and an "all done" date showing the date of the parents' return. Let the child check off a day every evening.
Joanna Keating-Velasco

4 Make the child's stay at home a mini-vacation by creating her own itinerary in a travel-brochure fashion. For each day, list and visually represent something fun (arboretum, bowling, ocean, hike, picnic etc.) so the child feels like she is on vacation, too. As you check off the child's itinerary, also check off a main calendar showing that the parents' trip is coming closer to an end, too.
Joanna Keating-Velasco

5 Create a chart that shows the child how many more school days or bed times until the traveling parent returns. You may have pictures of school under Monday, Tuesday, and Wednesday and a picture of mommy on Thursday when she is scheduled to come home.
Teresa Cardon

6 Let the child sleep with a t-shirt or pillow that belongs to the traveling parent. Familiar objects and smells can be very comforting.
Teresa Cardon

7 Have the parent who will be traveling read stories ahead of time and record them to create your very own "books on tape." Your child can listen to the tapes whenever he needs to feel close to the parent.
Teresa Cardon

8 Create an itinerary of the traveling parent's day with as much detail as appropriate. The stay-at-home parent can refer to the itinerary when the child asks, "Where is daddy?" If you can include pictures, it will be even easier to understand.
Michelle Pomeroy

9 Daily phone calls are a must. New computer gadgets can come into play here. Daddy can send a picture text, e-mail pictures, or both. There are also computer programs that allow you to communicate via camera so your child can chat live with the parent who is out of town.
Cindy O'Dell

10 Keep the routine as familiar as possible when a parent is away. It is disrupting enough to have the parent gone. Now is not the time to try a bunch of new recipes, hire a new respite worker, or go on trips to the zoo by yourself.
Teresa Cardon

Chores

1 To get the child to assist with emptying the dishwasher, place a sample of what goes where so he has a visual model and can work independently. For example, put a fork, spoon, and knife in the flatware caddy ahead of time as a model.
Mindy Small

2 Try gardening. First let the child go to the hardware store (if this is a positive thing for her) and pick out her own gardening gloves and tools. Also, have her pick out some flowers or tomatoes to plant. Depending on her skill, help her plant the flowers and dig in some soft soil for sensory fun. Later, keep a watering chart for caring for her flowers. Some kids really take this seriously. Their reward is their nice-looking garden or a favorite veggie.
Joanna Keating-Velasco

3 Fill a watering can with water and let the child water whatever he wants outside or direct him to certain areas. Give him a special area of the garden to be responsible for watering. Perhaps put in a little sign with his name on it.
Joanna Keating-Velasco

4 Make a huge visual chore board listing the names of all the children in your family. List household chores like setting the table and feeding the dog along with rewards, like read with mom and dad or computer time. Every day different family members rotate through different chores and rewards. Everyone knows what he or she is responsible for and gets special privileges all from one chart.
Cindy O'Dell

5 Use a mini schedule to break down the steps involved in the dog-feeding routine. Have your child check off each step as it is completed. Visually highlight the spot on the floor where the food bowl should be placed, using tape or a marker. Also, visually highlight the dog food bowl with a pen line or tape to show the child how much food to pour.
Mindy Small

6 "Clean your room" is not specific enough, nor even "Pick up everything up off the floor" – because then you'll find everything piled on the bed. Break the task down into steps. You can use a list or a picture schedule (some kids like to check the items off one by one).

For example, it might say something like:

☐ Pick up all clothing on floor and put in laundry basket.

☐ Pick up books and put on shelf.

☐ Pick up dirty dishes and take them to kitchen.

Kristi Sakai

If you're sure your child knows how to perform a household task, but he's reluctant, sweeten the deal and try a reward system. It doesn't have to be a tangible object. It can be watching a video or a TV program or doing a preferred activity together. For example, try saying, "Hurry up and clean your room so you can beat me playing *Sponge Bob Monopoly* again." See how much more quickly the child moves!
Kristi Sakai

Require that the dog be fed before the family meal is served in the morning and at night. Create a First/Then* visual reminder. One child can be in charge of changing the dog's water daily. Another sibling can feed the dog. This teaches teamwork and responsibility.
Joanna Keating-Velasco

Make three colored charts (each attached to a laundry basket) that match how you do laundry (one board has large bright color dots, the second has whites and creams, and the third has dark blues and blacks). Working with the child, sort the clothes into the appropriate color laundry basket. It's okay if they aren't perfectly sorted at first; you can fix it later. Some kids pick this concept up quickly (matching while doing a chore). Others may take a while, but meanwhile you are spending quality time together (while getting some chores done).
Joanna Keating-Velasco

Laminate a special paper placemat with a picture of a plate, fork, knife, spoon, and cup on it. Let it act as a guide for setting the table. Make enough for the whole family to have one so your child can help set the table for everyone.
Cindy O'Dell

CHAPTER 5

Summertime Fun

Summertime can be a difficult time for families and children alike. Routines get interrupted, and structure gets lost. But summer time can also be a time to create positive memories and family traditions. The tips that follow can help make summer a time to look forward to for both parents and children.

Summer Camp

1 Pack one complete outfit – shorts, shirt, socks, and underwear – in a gallon-size plastic bag. Bags can be labeled with a particular day of the week or left unlabeled, allowing the camper to choose his clothes for the day. Packing in a bag provides structure versus using a suitcase or a trunk where items can shift around.
Jill Hudson

2 Prepare a visual story that discusses various aspects of camp. This could include activities in which the camper has not previously engaged such as riding horses or canoeing, as well as new situations such as sharing a cabin with other campers or eating in the dining hall.
Jill Hudson

3 Create a collage or pack color photographs of family members and favorite things that the camper can hang by his bunk. These are helpful during lonely or stressful times.
Jill Hudson

4 Pack a transitional object – something that reminds the camper of home and gives him comfort while he is away from his familiar setting. (The object may become soiled, damaged, or broken, so choose carefully.)
Jill Hudson

5 Write a note to your camper for each day he will be away. Give the letters to the counselor to distribute during rest time each day.
Jill Hudson

Pack a disposable camera labeled with the camper's name. Tell the counselor that the camera exists and ask her to encourage the camper to use it.
Jill Hudson

Ahead of time, discuss activities that will occur at camp. Role play or talk about situations that seem difficult or are new, such as showering in an unfamiliar shower or sleeping away from home in a unknown bed. Advance preparation and determination of coping strategies for various situations will help prepare your camper and make for a smoother experience.
Jill Hudson

Have the child practice sleeping in a sleeping bag before camp. That way there is no issue the first night away from home. If the children are not bringing sleeping bags, find out what the sleeping accommodations are and plan accordingly.
Cindy O'Dell

Have the child practice walking at night with a flashlight outside in your backyard and playing with the flashlight in the dark of her bedroom.
Cindy O'Dell

Get brochures or pictures of the camp ahead of time and make a photo book for your child to look at before going. That way he has a better idea of what's going to happen.
Cindy O'Dell

Beach

1 If appropriate, study the tide pool schedule before going to the beach. (Buy a small tide pool book at the used-book store.) Go to the beach specifically to visit the tide pools and cross off critters that are shown in the book.
Joanna Keating-Velasco

2 Buy a sand castle tool/bucket set and create a town. Bring big cheap toy cars and figures to play with once the castle is built. You may have to get in the sand with your child.
Joanna Keating-Velasco

3 Look into surf lessons with an instructor who is willing to take extra time with your child. There are special programs, like Surfers Healing (surfershealing.org), for children with autism. This could be a holiday gift since it might cost some money and effort.
Joanna Keating-Velasco

4 Walk to the end of the pier and buy an ice cream cone. Sit on a bench and just enjoy the gorgeous ocean, dolphins, sea breeze, pelicans and silly seagulls.
Joanna Keating-Velasco

5 Bring a bottle of baby powder on trips to the beach. Once you put baby powder on sandy feet and hands, it cleans the sand right off.
Teresa Cardon

6 If your child doesn't like the sand, work on desensitizing him to sand before going to the beach. Introduce sand in small, less threatening ways, a cup full or bucket full at a time. Start with fingers and hands; then model putting your toes in. Graduate to larger containers and climb in. Be sensitive to your child's reactions and don't push too far too fast.
Teresa Cardon

7 Remember there are often limited resources at the beach, so pack plenty of food and drinks. Also, don't forget to have your child go to the bathroom before she heads way out onto the sand. If there are facilities at the beach, camp your stuff nearby and introduce the bathroom to your child before she has to go, so she is not overwhelmed and surprised when the time comes.
Teresa Cardon

8 Be prepared with a big umbrella or shade tent that can block the sun and the wind. Your child can still enjoy playing in the sand without the worry of sunburns and sand in his eyes.
Tiffany Fullmer

9 If your child does not like sunscreen or has sensitive skin, have him wear UV protective clothing. Don't forget a hat. Have the child practice wearing the hat and UV clothing in the backyard for several weeks before going to the beach.
Tiffany Fullmer

10 Create wet sand dribble castles using funnels and really wet sand. Put some sand and lots of water in a bucket. Take a small shovel or spoon and fill up the funnel with sand, then watch the sand dribble out of the funnel. You can create one-of-a-kind sand castles, and it is fun to watch the sand dribble out.
Tiffany Fullmer

Crafts and Outdoor Skills

1 Due to hypo-sensitivities in proprioception (sense related to being aware of movement and spatial orientation and the position of one's body – often subconscious), children with ASD may not get sufficient input to keep balance when riding a bike. Consider teaching the child to ride a two-wheeler on the grass – down a slight hill if necessary – so that the bumpy ride provides the needed sensory input. Plus, the grass is softer to fall on than pavement!
Stephen Shore

2 Create an obstacle course and invite the neighborhood kids over to join in the fun. You can use jump ropes to walk on or jump over, 4x4's for balance beams, hula-hoops to jump in and out of, and large blankets to roll on. It is great for gross-motor practice and social skill building as well.
Teresa Cardon

3 Use a trampoline for sensory input and to bounce off energy. If it gets too warm, put a sprinkler (be sure it is one that is low to the ground) under the trampoline and let the kids cool off while they jump. Be sure that NO ONE is allowed under the trampoline while people are jumping on top and, in general, exercise caution.
Teresa Cardon

4 Sprinklers can be a fun outdoor activity and a great opportunity for social interactions. Let your child choose a fun sprinkler (you can find sprinklers of Dora, Blues Clues, Sponge Bob, etc.). Start out slowly, and be sure that the first time you turn the water on your child is not surprised by the water. Then you can model (or better yet, have another child model) how to play with the water.
Teresa Cardon

5 Teach your child traditional summer time games like *Duck, Duck, Goose, Hide and Seek, Red Light, Green Light* and *Mother, May I?* Practice until the child can play the game with minimal prompting. Then invite one or two neighborhood kids over to play. Be available, if necessary, to facilitate the games so that everyone is involved and having fun.
Teresa Cardon

6 Buy cheap craft kits that are ready to go (check out the Oriental Trading Company for inexpensive materials; www.orientaltrading.com). You don't have to be "crafty" to use these products. They are also great craft ideas to donate to a child's teacher.
Joanna Keating-Velasco

7 Experiment with different media (clay, finger paint, pastel chalks, crayons, colored glue, play dough, poster paint, etc.) and see if your child takes an interest in any of them. If so, continue to pursue this interest using the chosen medium in various art projects.
Joanna Keating-Velasco

8 Hang up or display the finished crafts. Make a big deal about the things the child brings home from school. Use them as gifts for family members at holiday time.
Joanna Keating-Velasco

9 Go to a local kids' art studio and find out if it offers classes for which a relatively low number of kids are scheduled. Be frank about your child's needs when signing her up so that staff will be better able to offer support and accommodations. Prepare the child ahead of time by practicing the activity. If you can't attend with your child, have someone attend the class to assist the child (friend, sibling, or relative).
Joanna Keating-Velasco

10 Arts and crafts offer wonderful opportunities for the child to work on sequencing and following directions. Find activities (and even classes you can take with your child) at local craft stores. You can also find great craft ideas at www.familyfun.com. The key to helping your child be successful lies in creating a visual "recipe."*
Teresa Cardon

Swimming

1 Time spent around and in water should be safe and enjoyable. Keep a highly motivating item that can go in the water strictly for pool time. It doesn't have to be a toy. Lots of our children love bubbles; you can make all kinds of bubbles in the water.
Jeanine Nesvik

2 Watering cans make great pool toys; take turns filling the can and pouring the water out. Some kids like to watch the water pour out; others like the act of pouring. On the adult's turn, pour water on the child's arms, hands, legs – and eventually his head. Part of getting comfortable with water is allowing it to be in one's face, so pour the water in such a way that it runs down the child's face, but always be ready with a highly motivating toy or activity (the child's turn to pour the watering can, bubbles, song, etc.).
Jeanine Nesvik

3 Play washing machine. Holding the child in a basket hold, move her forward and backward and turn her whole body in a circle, saying "scrub, scrub, scrub" as you go around. Then comes the spin cycle, where you spin the child in one quick circle. Last is the dryer. Still holding the child in a basket hold, rock her back and forth like a baby. Be careful not to rock her too much because water may roll up onto her face (up the nose). The last thing we want is for the child to have a negative experience with the water.
Jeanine Nesvik

4 "Do This" is a phrase that many of our children learn when we teach them to imitate our actions. Use this phrase in pools and make it a game of splashing, blowing bubbles, putting face in water, or even just putting the mouth in the water. Keep the game fun – do two or three super-fun things for every one that takes the child outside his comfort zone. Example: If putting his face in the water is not as enjoyable as splashing, start with bubbles, stirring water with hands, kicking feet, then face in the water – and then lots of enthusiasm with splashing/slapping water. Motivation and the child's ability to be successful are the most important considerations here.
Jeanine Nesvik

5 Use the "Do This" phrase to help the child maneuver around the pool by wall walking (can also be called Spider-Man crawling, monkey walking, etc.) – hand-over-hand walking along the edge of the pool. Many children like to get back to the steps where they can stand/sit, so taking them a few feet away from the steps gives them motivation to get back. The first couple of times, move their hands for them; gradually assist less and less. Most children will hang on to the wall, but be ready for them to reach out or let go. Always put them back on the wall. Move toward the steps or sit on the steps; the child should not be out of your reach.
Jeanine Nesvik

6 When working in the water, always ensure routine and predictability. If the child enters the pool from the side (not the stairs/or shallow part where she can touch) – whether jumping to you, sliding in from a sitting position, etc. – immediately turn her toward the wall and have her grab the wall. From there the child can either wall walk to the steps or climb out of the pool. The routine of immediately reaching for the wall after entering the water is important in case the child ever falls into the pool unassisted.
Jeanine Nesvik

7 Use music and songs to establish routines. For example, pair songs with arm strokes, such as "Row-row-row your boat ..." Choose any favorite song while children are getting used to the feel of an assisted back float. This will give them a clear idea of what the upcoming activity is, and it also indicates how long the activity will last.
Jeanine Nesvik

Use favorite toys that float to turn the child's attention from the water to the toy. Play with the toy, have it float, swim under the water – whatever is fun for the child. As an incentive to move from the safety of the shallow water or the steps to a little deeper water, throw, or have the child throw, the toy a little distance out into the water. If the toy is motivating enough, the child will want to get it and reach for it before you get there; this makes it easy to hold the child in a horizontal position (Super-Man float/front float). This is a good way to get a fearful child to be so focused on the favorite toy that he stops clinging to your neck and starts reaching for the toy.

Jeanine Nesvik

Do as many things as possible that the child likes. Only add something outside her comfort zone a few times – and always do something super-reinforcing after the child tries or you help her try something new. End each session with something fun, and don't move too quickly: It's hard to recover from a frightening event in the water. Instead, go slowly and prevent one from happening in the first place. If something does scare the child in the water, the most important thing is for the caregiver not to get upset.

Jeanine Nesvik

It is important that children learn how it feels to float freely in the water. However, there is a time and a place for life vest/jackets:

- They need to be good ones – vests with belt that goes between legs (Coast Guard-approved ones are best).
- No water wings!!! They are unsafe, and it is too easy for the child to tip forward, forcing her face in the water, causing a very negative experience for the child.
- Start out by getting the child to be comfortable in the water without the jacket before introducing the jacket.
- Have split pool time with and without the jacket; too much time with jacket can cause a dependency and resistance to being in water without it.

Jeanine Nesvik

Things to Keep Them Busy

1 During the summer, join the summer reading program at the library. They have prizes and entertainment that kids love. Also check out the summer reading program sponsored by the Autism Asperger Publishing Company (www.asperger.net). It is both fun and informative.
Joanna Keating-Velasco

2 While summer is a time to let go, too much unstructured time can become overwhelming. Find a summer schedule that works for your family and then create visual supports to help your child know what to expect even on the new schedule. It can be as simple as a morning routine, outside time, arts and crafts, lunch, sensory play, water play, TV time, dinner and then the evening routine.
Teresa Cardon

3 Families worry about how to help their children maintain skills over the summer, so be sure to incorporate "learning" time into the summer routine. Take outside time, for example; if your child is working on matching colors, have several different colors of shovels available and match shovels as you dig in the sand. If your child is working on numbers or letters, be sure to play with sidewalk chalk while you work on the skill.
Teresa Cardon

4 Get creative with math facts. Find shells, sand toys, pool sticks, beach buckets, shovels, etc., and practice adding and subtracting the objects as you bury and uncover them in the sand. Or if your child prefers the water, find objects that sink and float and add and subtract as some stay afloat and others sink to the bottom.
Teresa Cardon

5 Summertime is also a great time to work on social skills. Sensory fun is a great way to do it. Water tables (or small wading pools) with collaborative activities are great for building social awareness. Place plastic fish in the pool and have everyone take turns catching a fish with only one fishing pole. Remember to include visual supports to help your child know when his turn is coming.
Teresa Cardon

6 Another great social opportunity is visiting summer hot spots: the zoo, museums, science centers, libraries, etc. These types of outings can be a huge challenge for kids with ASD, but a little prep work goes a long way. Take pictures of the venue ahead of time and create a story to go with them so the child knows what to expect once you get there. Maybe the trip to the zoo will involve seeing the elephant and the orangutans and then a ride on the merry-go-round – no more. Don't feel like you have to do it all in one shot.
Teresa Cardon

7 Don't forget: Summer is supposed to be fun. It will look different for every family. You know your child best, so plan the activities around his favorite things, and you will find a summer filled with happy memories.
Teresa Cardon

8 Post a calendar in a convenient place and have your child check it each day. Plan out the days and weeks with her ahead of time. Mark the calendar with activities, themes, days off, etc. For example, do dinosaurs for a week – go to the dinosaur museum, rent a dinosaur movie, make dinosaur-shaped sugar cookies, do dinosaur-themed play-acting, write poems and songs about dinosaurs, etc. Other weekly themes may include food (grocery

shopping, cooking, planning meals, etc.); personal care (visit a salon, paint nails, have a make-up play day, do stage make-up); outside (nature hike or hunt, types of flowers/birds, clouds, sun and moon cycles); local history; and entertainment (movies, swimming, parks).
Kathryn Jolley

Create a "day off" each week during the summer. Have your child build her own schedule on those days. She may choose to read all day, watch TV, or play with Barbies alone in her room. This gives the child some control over her schedule and environment. It also helps her learn to think ahead and make good choices based on her needs and wants at the time.
Kathryn Jolley

Kids' movies at the local movie theater are usually cheaper during the summer and are a great way to practice taking your child to the movies. Start out slowly. Maybe just attend one of the short cartoons before the feature film starts. A positive experience is the key.
Cindy O'Dell

CHAPTER 6

School Days

Many exciting and challenging things occur at school. Parents of children with autism spectrum disorders often feel anxious about the type of experiences their child may have in school. Two types of tips follow in this chapter: tips that are meant to provide ideas directly for parents and tips that parents may suggest to their child's educators to help ensure a positive educational experience and some consistency between home and school.

Bus Rides

1 To make a long ride to school more manageable, provide a list of street signs (for a reader) the bus will pass and have the child cross them off as they pass each one during the trip. For a non-reader, do the same but use photos of stores or buildings that the bus will pass.
Mindy Small

2 For long bus rides, send a Discman/iPod, etc., with the child to help pass the time.
Mindy Small

3 Use a raised cushion for a small child so he can better look out the bus window. He can keep the cushion in his backpack or leave it with the driver if he has the same bus driver each day.
Mindy Small

4 Send a favored/comfort object with the child to hold for the ride. If relinquishing it becomes a problem, provide the bus matron with a shoebox labeled "Finished" to put it in as the children exit the bus.
Mindy Small

5 Prepare the child for what to do and where to go if she misses the bus. Otherwise, in the event that the bus takes off without her at the end of the day, she might take it upon herself to walk home.
Joan Clark

Create a one-page visual support using pictures or words that remind your child of what activities he can do on the bus and what he cannot do. Laminate it and be sure to send it with him every day or, if possible, arrange to leave it with the bus driver if the same driver takes the child every day.
Teresa Cardon

Many children like maps and directions. Create a map of the route to school and add boxes along the way or landmarks that your child can check off during the ride. This is a good sequencing skill to practice; besides, it helps pass the time.
Teresa Cardon

Create a strategy to help your child make good choices when she is on the bus (or in class, on the playground, etc.), particularly when there isn't anyone else around to ask. Teach the child to think about three questions before doing something:
1. Is this something I would want to do?
2. Will I get in trouble for doing it?
3. Does this make sense?

Create a Power Card* that the child can take with her on the bus to remind her of the strategy.
Lisa Lieberman

Get to know your child's bus driver. He or she is with your child for a significant length of time each school day and can be an important member of your child's team. Be sure to share specific information about you child – calming activities, what may cause anxiety, favorite things, etc.
Teresa Cardon

Create a way for your child to monitor his behavior on the bus ride. A visual support that reminds him of the "rules" is a good start. Underneath the rules, add boxes where the child can put a check mark or smiley face. Make up rules for when the child gets to add a check mark, like every time the bus comes to a stop, or give him a watch to keep track of the time intervals.
Teresa Cardon

Handwriting

To help your child write within the lines, add a textural cue that he can feel when he passes over the line. Begin with a thick crayon line; if that's is not enough, use a piece of tape. Lastly, try a thin line of clay or play dough.
Mindy Small

To help with pencil placement within your child's hand, use a pencil grip. Using two hair elastics can help keep the pencil in place also. Knot a large one together with a smaller one (to make a funny-looking figure 8). Wrap the large one around the child's wrist and the small one around the pencil. The gentle pressure created this way not only keeps the pencil in the correct position, it may also provide comforting sensory input for your child.
Amy Misencik

For some children, pencils don't have enough weight to make them feel comfortable in their hand. Tape a couple of weights (nuts and bolts work well) on top of a pencil grip to provide more stability.
Teresa Cardon

Try lots of different types of pencils – mechanical, thick, thin, rounded, with grips, without grips, etc. – until you find one that fits the child. Be sure to share your child's preference with the school.
Teresa Cardon

Have the child write letters and words in the air with large hand movements. Use a flashlight or scarf to provide more input. Large movements may be easier for the child to perform than smaller ones.
Jenny Clark Brack

Use sidewalk chalk to practice letters, numbers, etc., or dip a paintbrush in water to draw on the chalkboard.
Jenny Clark Brack

Use a Magnadoodle™ or other drawing toy to practice writing and spelling words.
Jenny Clark Brack

Teach the child to type. In the world of computers, it is more important to be able type well than to have good handwriting skills. Basic ability to print letters is important, but beautiful penmanship is not.
Teresa Cardon

Find ways to motivate your child to practice handwriting skills. Shop with your child to buy wipe-off cards or practice books. Buy some that excite or interest. Also, buy colorful pencils, wipe-off markers or crayons. Practice together as a game or during one-on-one time; make it a fun reward instead of a chore. Hang the child's writings on the fridge or bulletin board and share them with others in a praising tone of voice.
Kathryn Jolley

Write with or in food. Create letters with cereal or cooked spaghetti noodles or peas. Draw letters in mashed potatoes or trace them in gravy. You can also use wipe-off placemats, and the child can follow the printed lines of each letter with her food items.
Kathryn Jolley

Homework # 1

1 Choose your battles wisely. Does the child wish to stand instead of sitting at her desk to do her work? If so, what's the harm? Make accommodations.
Stephen Shore

2 While the learning style of people with ASD tends to be visual, this is not true for everybody. If the child is a visual learner, make everything as visual as possible. If he is a kinesthetic (responds well to movement) learner, give him as many opportunities as possible to learn in a hands-on manner.
Stephen Shore

3 Teach your child to refer to a clock and/or watch to complete a task within a certain period of time. A visual timer, such as the Time Timer (see Appendix), is often helpful as the dial graphically shows how much time is left. Begin by having the child guess how long the task will take and then compare how long the task really took to accomplish.
Diane Adreon

4 Teach the child to be responsible for his belongings. Start with things such as keeping track of the toy train that he brought to grandma's house or took along in the car. Build into the routine that it is the child's responsibility to find the toy after the visit, carry it with him to the car, and bring it from the car into the house. Progress to items such as backpack and school supplies.
Diane Adreon

If the child feels overwhelmed when faced with a lot of homework problems, use a highlighter to show the exact problems she is responsible for completing. If your child understands a concept, it may not be necessary for her to complete 40 problems of homework. Talk with her teachers about accommodations that may include doing the even-numbered problems only or doing homework for a set number of minutes per night. These types of accommodations are important to bring up at IEP meetings so that there is documentation of the types of accommodations your child will be receiving.
Teresa Cardon

Many children on the autism spectrum have difficulty with transitions. Using two boxes or baskets, put a "Go" sign on one and a "Stop" sign on the other. The child is responsible to work the homework in the "Go" basket for an allotted length of time. When the time is up (use some type of timer to give a clear visual cue, such as Time Timer – see Appendix), the work goes directly into the "Stop" basket, and the child is finished with it for the day.
Teresa Cardon

Choose the same spot to do homework every day. Be sure that your child has a favorite pencil and eraser and that the homework routine stays the same.
Holly Reycraft

For some children, having a weighted lap blanket on their lap during homework time can help them stay focused by applying deep pressure.
Holly Reycraft

Let your child swing or participate in a sensory activity before starting homework. This will increase his ability to focus on the homework.
Holly Reycraft

Choose a homework time and location in your home that remains consistent from day to day. Your child will benefit from the routine and structure. Be sure it is an area free from distraction and that you are available to step in to help when asked.
Teresa Cardon

Homework #2

Here are some homework tips you may want to share with your child's teacher.

When assigning homework, base it on the amount of time you, as the teacher, want the student to do homework. Basing an assignment on number of problems completed may result in the student spending an inordinate amount of time on homework.
Brenda Smith Myles

Make sure that the homework assignment has a sample problem worked. If a parent has to work with her child on an assignment, it would be most helpful for the parent to know how the student was taught to complete the assignment.
Brenda Smith Myles

Review and sign a student's planner to ensure that all homework is listed. Having a parent sign the planner is also beneficial.
Brenda Smith Myles

Sometimes students with ASD have to be prompted to turn in their homework. Often they do the homework, but leave it in their locker or backpack.
Brenda Smith Myles

Develop a system with a parent that allows parents the flexibility to determine whether the student can do homework on a particular evening. Many students with ASD experience stress and anxiety associated with school and need the after-school hours to de-stress and relax.
Brenda Smith Myles

Some families who have a member with ASD cannot do homework with the child. If this is the case, provide a study hall for homework completion or have "no homework" designated on the student's IEP.
Brenda Smith Myles

Establish a method to communicate frequently with parents regarding the student's homework completion and homework grades. Parents may not be aware that their child has homework in one or more subjects.
Brenda Smith Myles

Provide a second set of textbooks for the student to keep at home. This prevents the student from having to carry books to and from school and also ensures the materials are available in case the student forgets to bring home a book.
Brenda Smith Myles

Provide a method for a student with ASD or her parent to confirm homework details and due dates. A website, buddy system, or email are all ways that help families verify whether or what type of homework the student may have.
Brenda Smith Myles

Many students with ASD have problems with handwriting. Provide alternate ways to complete assignments, including accepting typed assignments and projects instead of handwritten products.
Brenda Smith Myles

IEPS

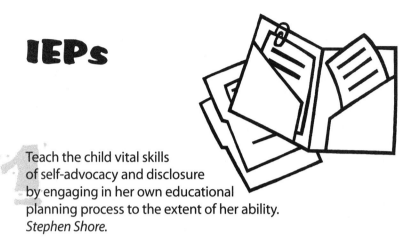

1 Teach the child vital skills of self-advocacy and disclosure by engaging in her own educational planning process to the extent of her ability.
Stephen Shore.

2 Don't feel you have to sign the IEP on the day of the IEP meeting. Take it home and review it word for word in a quiet place. Make sure you feel comfortable about the contract you are about to authorize. If you are unsure, ask questions and make changes until a satisfactory decision has been reached.
Prather Harrell

3 If your child is in a general classroom, work closely with the teacher to come up with a program that he will benefit from. Be clear and ask for accommodations that will support your child and the teacher. For example, your child may do better if he is seated near the front of the classroom. This way, if he gets distracted, the teacher can get his attention easily without disrupting the entire class. A simple tap on his shoulder may do the trick. Be sure to write accommodations such as specific seating arrangements into the IEP.
Amy Misencik

4 Bring a photograph of your child to the IEP meeting. It personalizes the process and serves as a visual reminder that the entire group has a central focus in mind.
Teresa Cardon

5 Do not go into the IEP meeting prepared to fight. You want to hear what everyone has to say, and you can't do that if you have already made up your mind. You don't have to make any decisions right at that moment, so listen with an open mind.
Teresa Cardon

Don't be afraid to bring someone else with you to an IEP meeting: a friend, neighbor, specialist, etc. Be sure to inform the school that you are bringing someone for moral support and to assist you in what can otherwise be an overwhelming process. This person doesn't have to be a professional advocate, just someone to help you write things down, think of questions to ask and, in general, be there for you.
Teresa Cardon

Not all IEP meetings go smoothly. Know your rights under the law (especially, the Individuals with Disabilities Education Act [IDEA]). Lots of websites, books, and parent groups (see Appendix for suggestions) can help you sift through the sometimes complicated laws related to special education.
Teresa Cardon

A great book with practical IEP tips and suggestions for parents is *Guns a Blazin'* (www.asperger.net). It is written for parents by a parent and isn't clouded with a bunch of legal terminology.
Teresa Cardon

Ahead of time, make a list of points you want to cover, goals you hope to implement, and questions you want to ask. It is easy to get off track during the meeting, and a list will help keep you on track.
Michelle Pomeroy

If you feel you are not getting anywhere with your school district, it may be time to look into next steps. Going to *due process* is your right (constitutional provision guaranteeing an accused person a fair and impartial trial). When parents file a complaint against a school district, they are requesting a hearing because they disagree with their child's current education plan. This is your right, but not one to be taken lightly. Be sure you have exhausted every other possibility and be honest and upfront with the district about your intentions.
Teresa Cardon

Informing and Teaching Peers About Autism Spectrum Disorders

Provide inclusive autism demystification programs and activities to promote an understanding of the characteristics of autism in an age-appropriate, fun, and sensitive manner.
Heather McCracken

If you plan to provide a peer training for junior high-age students, consider not being the presenter, observer or participant. Young teenagers seek independence. The presence of parents may be embarrassing and surely will be noticed by some unkind peers. Perhaps the training can be videotaped, if you want to see it.
Joan Clark

Don't do a disservice to typical peers or your child by assuming they know and understand autism. Go to the class and other-wise arrange to share information about the challenges and issues facing your child. Emphasize what likes or hobbies they have in common. Typical children want to learn about autism, and that knowledge helps them better interact with children on the spectrum.
Joanna Keating-Velasco

4 Use specialized books or programs (see the Appendix) as a discussion tool for introducing autism to elementary school kids. Tweak the discussion to fit the needs of your child. Decide as a family whether or not to include the child with ASD in the presentation.
Joanna Keating-Velasco

5 Donate a book about autism to the school library. See if the librarian will let you read it to the children on a scheduled day.
Joanna Keating-Velasco

6 Take the mystery out of autism and spend an afternoon discussing ASD with your child's friends. You can watch a child-friendly video or read a kid-friendly, discussion-oriented book (see the Appendix for ideas). Make sure to open up the discussion. Kids learn and understand a lot more that way.
Joanna Keating-Velasco

7 Find an autism demystification program (see the Appendix for ideas) that is easy to follow and has practical suggestions for teachers.
Teresa Cardon

8 Share information often. If you spoke with your child's peers in first grade, plan to do it again in second grade, third grade, etc. Remember, your child is changing all the time. Her likes and strengths as well as dislikes and areas of struggle should be updated with peers so that they can provide better support. There are also many changes in classrooms over the years, and you don't want to leave any peers out of the learning process.
Teresa Cardon

9 Read books written about autism for kids by kids. Books that are written from a child's perspective are often easy to read and easy to understand (see the Appendix for kid-friendly resources).
Teresa Cardon

10 Help peers understand different ways of experiencing the world by involving them in hands-on autism demystification activities (see the Appendix).
Teresa Cardon

Lunch Time

1. If possible, provide a lunch for your child that is similar to what peers at the lunch tables eat.
Joanna Keating-Velasco

2. Provide several healthy options even if the child chooses only one. Having options is good for independence. The unchosen options go home for the next day's choice. Limit the choices to two or three.
Joanna Keating-Velasco

3. Have the child pick an item weekly from the school cafeteria using the monthly menu. Waiting in line, choosing lunch items, and paying for lunch are great learning tools. An instructional assistant, teacher, or peer buddy can provide extra support as the child learns to navigate the school lunch system.
Joanna Keating-Velasco

4. Give your child food items that teach her independence. Can she open up her own drink or snack? If not, perhaps rethink and find snacks that she can eat without assistance.
Joanna Keating-Velasco

5. No one wants to eat alone. Be sure peer sensitivity training at school includes how the class is going to support the child on the spectrum at lunch. One of the best solutions is to have everyone eat together as a class. That way no one is left out, and everyone is participating in the social scene. Talk to your child's teacher about what is possible.
Teresa Cardon

Be sure that your child is using the appropriate utensils, napkins, etc., when eating. You don't want him to stand out for eating or behaving in ways that draw negative attention.
Teresa Cardon

Practice, practice, practice. The child with ASD needs to feel comfortable entering the lunch room, standing in line for food, finding a table, clearing his place, etc. Be sure that someone is assigned the role of practicing with him, whether a paraprofessional, a teacher, or a peer. And don't forget, if the lunch process changes, more practice will be needed.
Teresa Cardon

Create visual reminders on a small card to remind the child what is appropriate and what is not appropriate in the lunchroom. Reminders like hands to self, inside voice, my lunch only, walking feet, no throwing food, only throw away trash, no sharing food, etc., can go a long way toward making lunch a positive experience.
Teresa Cardon

Be sure to prepare your child for occasional alternate lunchtime plans, like eating in the classroom. Talk with your child's teacher to find out what alternatives are feasible and prepare stories that teach about these alternatives. Read the stories with your child often so that when the day arrives for lunch in the classroom or out on the playground, she will be prepared for the change.
Teresa Cardon

A school cafeteria is a noisy and crazy place. If your child is extremely sensitive to noise, have her eat outside at a park first, then try eating in a small room with several people. Slowly build until the child is capable of eating in a large space with more and more people. Eventually, she will make it to the cafeteria. Lunch is a social time, and we don't want the child to miss out on the experience entirely because of sensory overload.
Teresa Cardon

Paraprofessional Dos & Don'ts

Here are some tips that you can share with your child's paraprofessionals and teachers.

1 Always assume that the student is intelligent. Teach and speak with him as if he understands everything you say. Don't use huge words or speak quickly, but don't assume the student isn't intellectually aware simply because he is not using a typical means of communicating.
Joanna Keating-Velasco

2 Don't do too much for the student. It is better to break a large task down into tiny doable pieces than to do hand-over-hand on a larger task. The students get pride from completing a task or project on their own regardless of how many small tasks it takes to get there. Make sure to use the lowest possible prompting (gesture versus words).
Joanna Keating-Velasco

3 Be sure that the paraprofessional working with your child has been offered training and is receiving support from the school/ district. It is helpful to specify during the IEP process that training will happen for all staff members.
Teresa Cardon

4 Be sure that paraprofessionals understand that their role is to encourage independence. Paraprofessionals, in general, should not do anything for students that they can do for themselves.
Paula Kluth

Be sure that paraprofessionals know that, whenever possible, they should be looking for opportunities for peers to support, cue, and learn from students with ASD.
Paula Kluth

Paraprofessionals need clear guidelines on how to support students. Before working in the classroom and several times during the year, the paraprofessional should have opportunities to watch teachers or therapists perform their job duties. In addition, the paraprofessional should be observed by teachers and/or therapists often. This is not for the sake of evaluating performance as much as it is to coach the individual and help him or her refine skills and develop new competencies.
Paula Kluth

One of the most pivotal things for a paraprofessional to understand is the relationship between behaviors and consequences. Paraprofessionals need to know that they are reinforcing appropriate behaviors and not reinforcing inappropriate behaviors. They should be a part of the process when putting together intervention plans because they are often the key player implementing the plan.
Teresa Cardon

A great resource to share with your child's school, teachers and paraprofessional's is *How to Be A Para Pro: A Comprehensive Training Manual for Paraprofessionals* by Diane Twachtman-Cullen (see the Appendix).
Teresa Cardon

It is important that paraprofessionals be trained in how to help a child with ASD navigate peer interactions. It is also important that they learn how to fade out of social interactions as quickly as possible. It needs to be all about the peers, and not all about the adults!
Teresa Cardon

It is a good idea for paraprofessionals to help other children in the classroom at some point. The child with ASD needs to know that she is not the only one who requires extra support. Similarly, peers in the classroom shouldn't feel like the paraprofessional is "off-limits" to them.
Teresa Cardon

Reading

1 Think about reading as being comprised of two parts, decoding and comprehension. *Decoding* refers to the ability to sound out letters and read words; *comprehension* is the ability to attach meaning to what is read. Read with and to your child as often as possible.
Anthony Koutsoftas

2 To teach letter/sound recognition, consider purchasing/borrowing videos dealing with phonics (see the Appendix).
Amy Misencik

3 When practicing reading with a reluctant reader, find out the child's main interests. Find books six months to one year below the child's reading level. A high-interest book at the child's recreational or comfort level will help make reading fun and at the same time increase the child's comprehension. If necessary, ask for advice from your child's teacher.
Caroline Levine

4 When working on reading comprehension, read familiar books that contain a story plot, meaning that there is a clear problem and solution to the story. Books like *Brown Bear, Brown Bear* or the *Spot the Dog* series do not provide children with exposure to the concept of a story, and while they are fun for beginning readers, they do not have enough of a story plot to effectively work on comprehension. Instead, choose stories that have a clear beginning, middle, and ends when working on comprehension. Books with simple, familiar plots are more effective when the focus is on a child's reading comprehension skills.
Anthony Koutsoftas

5 Read books that are part of a series so that the characters become familiar. This is good for two reasons. You can compare and contrast how the characters behave in each of the stories and the child will be able to carry familiar information about the character from one book in the series to the next.
Anthony Koutsoftas

6 Ask one Wh-question per page and make sure to vary the questions. Consider using the five-finger Wh-question approach. Each finger on your hand becomes a Wh-word (Thumb=Who; Forefinger=What; Middle Finger=Where; Ring Finger=When; and Pinky = Why). After you read the first page of a book, ask a "Who?" question and close your thumb. After reading the next page, ask a "What?" question and close your forefinger, etc.
TIP: It is O.K. to ask easy questions that involve pointing, in addition to difficult questions like why?
Anthony Koutsoftas

7 Don't stay with one book for too long. Children have their favorite books that they want read over and over because they are familiar and comfortable. Make sure that you are always introducing new books. One way is to bring the child to the bookstore or library to pick out a new book. Another suggestion is to read the new book after reading a familiar book so the transition to the new book is a bit easier.
Anthony Koutsoftas

8 Make or buy puppets to represent the characters in a given story and act out the story with the puppets as you go. This will help give the story a three-dimensional feel and eases comprehension. You can also bring the puppets in the car or on appointments and re-enact stories that your child has read.
Anthony Koutsoftas

9 Creating adaptive literacy books not only encourages a greater interest in books for a reluctant reader but aids in comprehension, too. Add pictures, like rebus symbols*, to familiar children's stories or create your own stories using a picture software program (see the Appendix). Point to the words and pictures as you read.
Teresa Cardon

10 Create interactive books on your computer. You can find great examples on the Internet (http://speech.jppss.k12.la.us/archives. htm or http://www.dltk-kids.com). Be sure to include visual pieces that your child can Velcro to the book and practice taking turns with.
Teresa Cardon

Special Interests and Downtime

USE SPECIAL INTERESTS!!!! When teaching counting, instead of counting wood blocks, count Big Bird figures or toy vacuum cleaners. When the child is learning to identify colors, instead of using colored discs, use varying color trains or colored Dora the Explorer figures.
Mindy Small

For reading/comprehension activities, replace the main character with a main character from the child's special interest (e.g., Boy writing home to mother, replace boy with Luke Skywalker and mother with Queen Amadala from *Star Wars*).
Josie Santomauro

Find ways to use special interests and passions to connect with others for success in social interaction, developing friends and relationships, as well as involvement in the community. For example, if your child likes computers, find a computer class or club in the community that she can join.
Stephen Shore

Use the power and motivation behind the child's special interests as a way of expanding his education. For example, a focused interest on airplanes may be employed to learn geography by discussing where planes go; mathematics is learned as distance, fuel use, and travel time are calculated. Possible career opportunities surrounding airplanes may also be explored.
Stephen Shore

Include a "word of the day" in your child's lunchbox. Cut out a picture of something and write the word underneath. It is a fun way to teach new words and expand your child's vocabulary.
Amy Misencik

A fun visual reward system is to create a puzzle from a picture of your child's special interest (Disney princesses, dinosaurs, trains, etc.). Print the picture on cardstock and laminate it. Cut out pieces so they can be put back together like a puzzle. Every time the child engages in on-task behavior, completes math problems, etc., he earns a puzzle piece. Kids love to watch as a picture of one of their favorite things takes shape.
Teresa Cardon

Ask your child's teacher if there is a leisure cupboard at school with stuff the kids can use during downtime. Some kids on the spectrum need a place to go since "leisure" is a foreign concept for them. If there is no such cupboard, ask the teacher if she would mind if you sent a note to all of the parents requesting three leisure activities their child likes (sensory balls, Magic 8 Ball, Etch-a-Sketch, books, CD players, etc.). Collect them in a laundry basket and give them to the teacher. At the end of the year, you can ask for them back or donate them to this teacher's care.
Joanna Keating-Velasco

Before school starts, talk with your child's teacher about things that the child finds calming. This may include some issues of *Sports Illustrated*, a spinning chair, access to swings, a cozy corner, or whatever your child finds calming. You want the teacher to have things ready for when your child gets overwhelmed and needs some downtime.
Teresa Cardon

Many children find it difficult to decide what to do during free time. Providing a list of visual or written choices can be incredibly helpful.
Teresa Cardon

Recess is often a time for kids to wind down and relax. While activities during recess to support social skills are great, remember that sometimes just sifting sand for a few minutes can do a lot for an overwhelmed sensory system.
Teresa Cardon

Teaching

The following are some suggestions that may be beneficial for your child's teacher. Share as appropriate.

ALWAYS use a visual schedule* – whether using pictures or written words. Save a favored activity or a choice activity for last.
Juliane Hillock

Use concrete language. Don't rely on verbal directions. Write the directions on the board and have the student repeat them back. Have a model already completed to demonstrate the end result. Use a familiar format.
Juliane Hillock

For some students, fidgeting promotes attending to activities/instruction, including doodling, rocking in a chair, or holding a toy. Have a fidget box available that includes small items (squishy ball, putty, pipe cleaner, etc.) for the student to use when she needs to pay attention to a speaker, for example.
Jenny Clark Brack

Do some wake-up activities before seatwork. This includes finger plays, calisthenics, running in place, jumping, stretching, push-ups on chair or desk, moving furniture (putting down chairs), etc.
Jenny Clark Brack

Schedule activities so that periods of sitting are alternated with periods of movement, such as getting a drink, going to the bathroom, handing out papers, taking a note to the office, etc.
Jenny Clark Brack

Help students anticipate the day's activities, especially when there are changes to the routine. A visual schedule* is helpful. Pictures and symbols can provide information (place on desk, blackboard, wall or in a small book) to help with transitions.
Jenny Clark Brack

Try some or all of the following to deal with sensory issues: decrease wall decorations, adjust lights, provide a table easel and window guide for reading, offer adapted handwriting paper, decrease copying from the board in favor of copying from a page or book at close range, thicken cutting lines, outline coloring picture with glue or some other material for clearer boundary and tactile input.
Jenny Clark Brack

Some students resist putting pencil to paper because of difficulties with handwriting. In such instances, allow the child to use assistive technology. Try switching to a portable keyboard or to a computer. In addition, some students are interested in the many options available in Microsoft Word (e.g., typing in different colors and fonts).
Paula Kluth

Experiment with different writing materials. Students may be motivated to produce more when they are using markers, colored pencils, or novelty pens such as those that are oversized, filled with water, or bendable.
Paula Kluth

Give the student a camera and let him take photos around his home, in the classroom or at a special event. The photos can serve as visual cues for writing a story, play, letter, poem, or manual. This process works best if the photos follow some sequence or are related in some way (e.g., the beginning, middle, and end of a baseball game, the feeding of the class pet).
Paula Kluth

CHAPTER 7

Community Events and Outings

unning errands or otherwise spending time in the community with your child in tow can seem daunting for fear of causing behavioral outbursts. The following tips help you prepare ahead of time and offer specific strategies to use when you are out and about so that you and your child can navigate the community more smoothly and with greater enjoyment.

Grocery Shopping

1. Create a picture "sublist" of your shopping list with items the child can find along the grocery shopping route. Let him pick the item. Don't interrupt the choice process. Who cares if you end up with a different brand of cheese once in a while?
Joanna Keating-Velasco

2. On your own, walk through the grocery store, aisle by aisle, and create a comprehensive list of items you normally buy. Put the items into a spreadsheet on the computer and turn them into a list that you can just check off each week. When you shop aisle by aisle using this list, you won't have to go back to an aisle because you missed something. Some children on the autism spectrum don't like backtracking. An organized list can solve this dilemma.
Joanna Keating-Velasco

3. During the week, let the child earn money for doing basic chores. Make sure to prompt him to bring the money in a wallet to the store. When you go to check out, if he wants a bag of candy, check to see if he brought his wallet. If not, do not buy the candy. Of course, you have to use baby steps to work up to this process.
Joanna Keating-Velasco

4. Let the child help pick out items for her lunch while at the store. Give her a choice of two if choosing is a hard concept for her. Hold up the items and say, "Pick one."
Joanna Keating-Velasco

Make a picture grocery list with your child to take to the store. Make sure to include pictures of foods that your child prefers. Alternate preferred items with other items to be purchased, saving a favorite for the end of the list. By doing so, you are encouraging your child to shop for all items with you in order to get that most desired item at the end of the list.
Amy Bixler Coffin

Keep trips short at first. Just buy one or two items and leave the store.
Cindy O'Dell

If your child can handle longer periods of shopping, give her tasks to do in the store. For example, putting items in the cart or looking for specific things. Always reward the job with a prize at the end. The reward doesn't have to be candy! It could be half an hour of watching a favorite show (which is well-planned downtime after the shopping trip).
Cindy O'Dell

Shop during the slow parts of the day to avoid crowds and long lines at check-out.
Cindy O'Dell

Plan times to go shopping without other siblings. This way you will be 100% focused on your child on the spectrum so you can make it a positive experience.
Cindy O'Dell

Give your child something to do that will take his mind off the boring task of grocery shopping. If safe, send him on a scavenger hunt and look for things throughout the store. For example, he can try to find as many green things or things with the letter "T" on them as possible while walking up and down the aisles with you. If the child likes to write or draw, give him a pad of paper and ask him to record the things he sees.
Teresa Cardon

At the Dentist's

Find a dentist (use referrals from classmates' parents) who specializes in treating kids with ASD. Enough said!
Joanna Keating-Velasco

Ask if the dentist will let your child "wear" the X-ray robe during the appointment to apply a calming pressure to his body.
Joanna Keating-Velasco

Call in advance to share information about the child's needs and strengths and to obtain information about the event for which you are scheduled.
Jill Hudson

In the waiting room, create an environment that is calming to your child (headphones with favorite music, comfort object, DVD player, handheld video games, fidget toys, etc.). Helping him to stay relaxed and at a low level of anxiety will help him transition and better engage in the future steps of the appointment.
Jill Hudson

Ahead of the appointment, ask for a sample of the small X-ray film dentists use. Let your child practice with the X-ray film and a mirror at home before the visit to get familiar with the shape and feel in her mouth.
Teresa Cardon

Relaxing music playing through headphones is a must in the dentist office. The noise of the drill is worrisome even if it is just being overheard from the office next door.
Teresa Cardon

Watch videos and read stories with your child about trips to the dentist ahead of his appointment. Let the child experiment with small mirrors, toothbrushes, and rubber gloves (keeping safety and allergies in mind) to familiarize him with the experience.
Teresa Cardon

Take your child to the dentist for a visit where nothing happens in his mouth. Let the child get familiar with the sounds, sights and smells of the office. Call ahead and make sure this is okay. If it isn't, you might want to find a new dentist.
Teresa Cardon

Take pictures of the dentist, the technicians, receptionists, the chair, the X-ray machine, etc., and create a personalized story* about what your child can expect when going to the dentist. Be sure to end the story with a picture of the rewards he will receive (from either you or the dentist) when the visit is over.
Teresa Cardon

Portable DVD players are great for keeping your child's mind off things. Bring her favorite show to play. If the dentist has a screen for movies, ask his staff to put in your child's favorite show. Keeping her favorite DVD on hand can be VERY helpful.
Cindy O'Dell

Doctor's Appoint- ments

1 If you know your child will be difficult to manage and want to be sure there is plenty of staff to help out, let the doctor know a head of time. Just because it says autism in the child's chart doesn't mean the staff will know to anticipate behavioral and other issues. It also may help to schedule early-morning or late appointments when the office and staff are not so occupied and can devote more attention to your child.
Hunter Manasco

2 As mentioned for dental appointments, call in advance to share information about your child's needs and strengths and to obtain information about the procedure for which you are scheduled.
Jill Hudson

3 Create an environment that is calming to your child. Keeping him relaxed and at a low level of anxiety will help him transition and better engage in the future steps of the appointment.
Jill Hudson

4 Doctors and other health professionals often wear scrubs and white coats. Wear scrubs or white lab coat while at home playing with the child at one of his favorite activities to get him used to the look and feel.
Juliane Hillock

5 Get a doctor kit and play doctor at home. When you go to the doctor, bring the kit along. Have the child "play doctor" as the doctor

checks you or whoever out. Most doctors are accommodating and more than happy to get into the act.
Cindy O'Dell

Help your pediatrician establish a relationship with your child by providing treats that are reinforcing for your child. When you visit the doctor with your typical children, the doctor can perform the checkup on them as usual while quietly handing your child with ASD a reinforcer. Each time you visit the doctor, have him or her make an attempt to talk with your child or touch him (pat his head or give a high five) and provide a reinforcer. That way, when your child gets sick, he is more likely to be at ease and trust the doctor.
Cindy O'Dell

If your child has a condition that requires specialized equipment, such as a breathing treatment machine, try to start treatments at home. Easing into the treatment and receiving it at home first makes the doctor visit less scary.
Cindy O'Dell

If you are bringing several children in for checkups, let siblings be checked out first. That gives your child a role model to follow.
Melissa Van Hook

When you are making an appointment, be very clear that you will need a little extra time and explain why. This way the office staff can schedule you during a time that tends to be more flexible if you need more time (for example, the last appointment of the day, the first of the day, the one before or after lunch).
Cindy O'Dell

Give your child a visual schedule* to let her know what will happen on the visit to the doctor. Include waiting in the waiting room, standing on the scale, having her temperature taken, waiting again in the exam room, the doctor coming in and checking her ears, chest, etc. Your child may prefer having a way to check off the different steps, so bring a pen or marker along. Be sure to include a reward at the end of the schedule so the child has something to look forward to.
Teresa Cardon

Haircuts

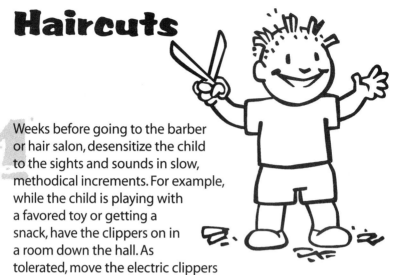

1 Weeks before going to the barber or hair salon, desensitize the child to the sights and sounds in slow, methodical increments. For example, while the child is playing with a favored toy or getting a snack, have the clippers on in a room down the hall. As tolerated, move the electric clippers closer, eventually bringing them in the same room. Then as the child tolerates being near the clippers while they are on, run a soft brush, then a comb and, finally, the guide to the clippers through the child's hair. Only do what the child tolerates. Move back a step and try again if the child seems distressed.
Juliane Hillock

2 Haircuts may be difficult due to the buzzing of the cutters, the light touch of the person cutting the hair, or even the pulling of the hair on the scalp as it is being shorn off. Consider using pictures to prepare for the haircut, providing a distraction such as a Gameboy or other favorite activity, and provide frequent breaks.
Stephen Shore

3 Get a reference from someone in your child's class or support group for a hair stylist who is good with kids with ASD. Make a sequence chart* for the hair appointment (wait, greet stylist, wash hair, cut hair, blow dry, pay, reward) depending on how much visual assistance your child needs. Tip the stylist well and you will see a smiling stylist on your next visit.
Joanna Keating-Velasco

Go near closing time so no unexpected hair dryers are turned on by other stylists.
Renata Irving

Ask the stylist to put the drape on your child backwards so his arms are free in the front but he is still covered. Tell him it is his cape "like Batman."
Renata Irving

Tell the stylist that you are counting backwards and that she has to stop at 1, no matter what. This means that the priorities must be done first – bangs, sides and back length. Final styling can be done *if* there is time (be sure to say all this before the cape goes on and you start counting).
Renata Irving

Let the child hold the clippers or have the stylist put it on your arm to show it is a safe tool and won't hurt.
Renata Irving

Bring an extra t-shirt for the child to put on after the cut so she won't feel uncomfortable if hair touches her body. Always go home to wash up immediately afterwards.
Renata Irving

Massage the child's scalp prior to haircuts. This will help her prepare for the stimulation she will feel from the haircut. It can also help her relax.
Jenny Clark Brack

Keep it simple. Looking at everything around the stylist's station can be overwhelming, even scary. If there is an empty station without flat irons, blow dryers and styling products lying around, ask if your child can sit there to reduce the chance of overstimulation.
Teresa Cardon

Community Outings

1 If your child does not want to get in the car to run errands with you, let her bring something special along. Keep a tote bag by the garage door and give the child the bag to take to the car. She can even help pack the bag the night before. That way she will always have a favorite treat along.
Jennifer Frandsen

2 Have your child get his own library card. Put "library" on your weekly schedule and follow through by going to the library. Check out the same number of books each week to make returning books easier. Have a bin at home strictly for library books.
Joanna Keating-Velasco

3 If your child loves a sport such as gymnastics, swimming, or tae kwon do but has problems paying attention in a class setting, start out with private lessons. Every now and then, have another child join the class, but keep it to no more than two students. The price is a bit higher, and your child will not start out benefiting from the peer interactions, but he will get plenty of physical stimulation and he will learn to enjoy the activity. Sometimes it's important to let our children just have fun.
Amy Misencik

Before going to the mall, create a "treasure hunt" check-off list of mall stores using photos of their logos or storefronts. This way, the child has an activity to keep his interest while strolling in the mall with you. Once he has checked off all the stores, have the last store be a reward store (the ice cream counter or the pet shop).
Joanna Keating-Velasco

Before visiting a museum, go on line or get a book related to the exhibits of the museum. Create a treasure hunt in pictures of things the child is to locate on your visit. Leave an area for checking off each item. If you can talk to a curator (or refer to a floor plan) and keep the hunt items in a flowing order, this will help you move steadily through the museum. Perhaps the last item on the list is the museum store where the child can pick out one item if his list is complete.
Joanna Keating-Velasco

Write a few social rules about visiting the public library on a cue card*. Pair a picture with each rule. Read over the rules several times before going to the library. When needed, quietly show your child the picture/s to remind her of the rules when she is at the library.
Amy Bixler Coffin

Get to know the children's librarians at your local library and tell them about your child's special needs. They will be more understanding and willing to make accommodations if they understand her challenges. Go early in the morning before the library gets busy. The children's librarian might even let you go into a reading room after your child has picked out books. Your child could then enjoy going through the books, or you can read to her.
Joanna Keating-Velasco

Do a lot of previewing before visiting new, and sometimes even familiar, sites. Go to the website of the location. Show the child pictures of the site, including the places and things he is sure to visit and can look forward to (e.g., boa constrictor, submarine exhibit, assembly line). Some venues such as museums and parks have videos that are given away free, streamed on their websites or available for a nominal fee.
Paula Kluth

Get a menu from a local café, ice cream parlor, or smoothie bar and help your child choose a favorite item that he would like to purchase. Then help him determine the amount of money needed to purchase the item. Head to the location and let your child order and pay for the item. It is great to practice this often.
Michelle Pomeroy

Make accommodations for your child. When you are at a restaurant, the library, the pool, etc., sit near a door or exit. If your child looks like he is on overload, take breaks. Go to the bathroom, step out in the hallway or some other place, and let him have a break.
Cindy O'Dell

Tools for Taking Your Child's Mind off Difficult Tasks

"Magic Wand" or Glitter Stick – Hold the wand upright, so all the glitter is at the top. Have the child focus on the glitter, take a deep breath and blow onto the stick to make the glitter fall towards the bottom. Flip the stick upside down and repeat. Obviously, the glitter will eventually fall on its own due to gravity, but engaging the child in this blowing activity empowers him as he makes a difference in the function of the glitter, relaxes his body because he is taking deep breaths and focuses his attention on an activity instead of the anxiety he is experiencing.
Jill Hudson

Blowing Bubbles – This activity serves several functions. It allows the child to take deep breaths as he blows the bubbles, which naturally relaxes his body. It also gives him a focus as he tries to pop the bubbles that are floating by. If popping the bubbles is easy for the child, ask him to try to catch one with the bubble wand. The disappearance and reappearance of the bubbles can be paralleled to the coming and going of the professionals (doctors, nurses, dentists, etc.). Remind the child that staff members will appear and

go away and come back again and again. Also remind the child that even if you are asked to leave (because you are not allowed in the treatment room or the operating room), you will reappear just like the bubbles.
Jill Hudson

I SPY Book – Hold the book for the child while she is engaged in a challenging task. Ask her to locate an object on a given page. If the child is unable to use her hands to point to the picture, ask her to describe what else is next to it so that you can point it out on her behalf.
Jill Hudson

"What Am I?" – Describe an object or person to the child, revealing only one clue at a time. Have the child guess who or what you are thinking of based on a combination of all of the clues you have provided. Then allow the child a turn to think of a person or object and give you clues as well.
Jill Hudson

Positions of Comfort – The way in which a child is positioned or held during a medical or other procedure can make a big difference. For example, when going to the dentist, allow the child to sit on your lap, while you wrap your arms around the front of the child comfortably holding his arms down. Encourage the child to recline on you and relax.
Jill Hudson

Thinking of Something Else –Try giving a simple hand or shoulder massage or playing soothing music or a favorite video if you have a portable DVD or laptop. This may help to distract the child's attention as well as calm him in general. Verbal games can help, too. Probably the most widely used way of getting through injections is asking the child to guess what exciting thing you will do after the shot. Thinking of what it could be, speaking aloud, and the positive emotions associated with doing something fun make for a good combination for momentarily distracting a high-functioning child and minimizing her perception of pain.
Hunter Manasco

"Give Yourself a Hand" – Fill inexpensive knit gloves with scented rice and close the tops using hot glue so the rice stays in. For children who need to be aroused during group activities where they are required to wait their turn, put peppermint, tangerine or lemon scent in the rice. For children who need calming, put in lavender. Choose colors of gloves that match the purpose (e.g., red or orange for arousal; blue or green for calming). Store in resealable plastic bags with the child's name on the bag for sanitary purposes. Cold is good for arousal; for children who need calming, use gloves at room temperature or put them in microwave to warm slightly.
Glenda Fuge

Rewards Are Not Bribes – Children on the spectrum often do better if they have something tangible to work for. Give teachers, doctors, nurses, etc., permission to offer a reward. Find what motivates the child and let him earn it. You can distract the child from upsetting visits to the doctor or hair salon if he is thinking about a reward instead of the stressful situation.
Cindy O'Dell

Twenty Questions – When you are waiting in places like at a restaurant or a doctor's office and your child gets bored, play *Twenty Questions* using her special interest. Focus questions on Disney movies or whatever your child loves to talk about.
Lisa Keegan

Fidget Toys – Keep fidget toys in your purse, pocket, or car and replenish them often. If your child gets antsy in line somewhere, or needs a distraction of some sort, pull out the fidget. They can be live savers.
Teresa Cardon

Waiting Rooms

Waiting time can make your child anxious, but her anxiety can be relieved somewhat if she knows what will happen. Provide her with a sequence of events*; if possible, include a picture reminder of a later reward for cooperation. If it is a common event, you can print off an actual schedule, but in a pinch you can easily make one on the spot. A list of quickly drawn picture sequence might include:

- check in with receptionist
- nurse calls your name
- go to room in the back where the nurse weighs and takes vitals
- see the doctor
- wave good-bye
- stop at drive-through for ice cream. The ice cream can be a reward for reasonable (but not perfect) behavior and cooperation.

Kristi Sakai

Always think ahead and be prepared with everything you might need to have with you AT ALL TIMES. A few suggestions include water bottle, handheld electronic or other small game (especially enticing if only used for waiting times), pen and paper to make a quick visual aid or checklist, snacks, CD or MP3 player with headphones, earplugs, a small blanket (to allow your child to cover his head if he's overwhelmed), healthy but fun snacks (granola or protein bars, jerky, fruit leather, apple chips).

Kristi Sakai

3 Bring along activities that can be done in a quiet and sedentary environment. For example, read a book, color a picture, play a board game or listen to music. Provide the child with a series of simple, visual pictures for the activities that are available at a particular moment. Not all pictures need to be a choice at every point.
Jill Hudson

4 Explain the non-negotiables versus the choices that are available, such as "Right now we have to sit in the waiting area, but you can choose which activities you would like to do while you wait."
Jill Hudson

5 Don't expect the child to sit perfectly still while waiting. His body may need to move to relieve some of his anxiety. Unless he is directly getting into another person's space (or is sick), let him walk in circles, flap, or rock to keep relaxed. If such behaviors help your child feel better, ignore any curious looks they may provoke from others.
Kristi Sakai

6 Use a countdown of numbers* to indicate that the time in the waiting area, and for the chosen activity, continues to decrease. Periodically remove the next highest number in the sequence until all of the numbers are gone. The numbers do not necessarily equal a minute. Be sure to check in with the front desk attendant periodically to coordinate the amount of time remaining versus removal of the countdown numbers.
Jill Hudson

7 Don't lie to your child by saying a procedure won't hurt, if you know it will. Prepare him ahead of time and tell the truth, but stress the reason for the procedure and the reward he will receive afterwards. If you lie to get it over with, he won't believe you next time. And as you have years of doctor's visits ahead of you, lying will only make things harder in the long run.
Kristi Sakai

8 Review simple pictures of the steps in which the child will participate or the equipment the child will encounter, such as a stethoscope, blood pressure cuff, etc. Explain each step and determine (a) if the child has any questions, (b) which steps he considers difficult, and (c) which steps he thinks will be easy.
Jill Hudson

9 Give the child a role to play. Define her job as she participates in the upcoming appointment. This may be as simple as sitting as still as a statue or just breathing in and out. Practice the child's role with her and praise her even during the waiting period. This reaffirms that she can be successful during the actual appointment.
Jill Hudson

10 If it stresses your child out too much to wait in the waiting room, tell the receptionist that you will be waiting out in the hall (or out-of-doors if need be). A staff member will come to find you when it is time for your appointment. They would much rather start your child's appointment when your child is regulated and content than make him stay and get stressed and upset in the waiting room.
Teresa Cardon

CHAPTER 8

Holidaze!

olidays and special events can be an overwhelming time for everyone, but they are integral parts of establishing family traditions, so don't just avoid them because you know they will be challenging. Prepare your child so that she can manage the changes in routine that are inevitable and, ultimately, learn to enjoy and look forward to holidays and special events.

Birthdays

The concept of birthdays can be tricky. To help your child understand that he is now a year older, have his peers and teachers help out. Find a t-shirt and write on the front of it with a permanent marker "Look out ... I'm 5!" Then on the back of the shirt write, "I'm the birthday boy!" After hearing "Happy Birthday!" and "Wow! You're 5!" all day, your child will get the idea.
Amy Misencik

Make sure the party is planned around what the child wants – not just a traditional party full of sensory chaos. If you do plan a more traditional party, have break areas, sensory tables, quiet zones, wide selection of food, etc.
Joanna Keating-Velasco

Find out what the child is totally into and make that the theme of the party. If he likes bulldozers, go to a construction site and ask the foreman to take him around the site and ride the bulldozer. If he likes whales, go on a whale-watching trip. If he likes trucks, rent a truck. If she likes Disney princesses, see if you can hire someone to come dressed as Snow White to your house.
Joanna Keating-Velasco

Keep it simple! This includes the number of guests, the games, the food, etc. This is especially important if your child is too young to understand what a birthday is.
Teresa Cardon

Use your child's special interest as the theme for the party. It is a great way to keep her motivated, and every game and activity becomes a treat rather than a chore.
Teresa Cardon

If your child's diet or food preferences do not permit cake, choose any other dessert that is appropriate for him. Remember it is his special day.
Teresa Cardon

Before the big day, make some frosted cupcakes and practice with your family singing Happy Birthday and the child blowing out the candles.
Cindy O'Dell

Have the child practice opening wrapped toys so she gets used to opening presents. She can also practice saying "thanks" and other appropriate comments that go along with receiving gifts.
Cindy O'Dell

Start with a small birthday party. Invite your immediate family and maybe one or two other kids. Decorate and do games like a piñata and *Pin the Tail on the Donkey*. Help your child a lot throughout the party. Keep it short and sweet.
Cindy O'Dell

It's O.K. to turn down invitations to parties you know will be crowded or loud. If appropriate, consider having your child bring a gift and a cupcake to sing "Happy Birthday" and leave early. This way you are still working on the birthday theme with your child.
Cindy O'Dell

Annual Holidays

The tips suggested for holidays below may be adjusted to special holidays and events your family celebrates.

Work with your child on the computer to create personal Valentines. He will learn computer skills, and you will get quality one-on-one time with him. Don't forget to give the aides a Valentine. Include a recent photo if possible.
Joanna Keating-Velasco

Remember that kids in the class might have special dietary needs. Check with the teacher before sending candy for the other students to share. The only thing worse than not being able to eat chocolate is to receive it as a gift and then not be able to eat it!
Joanna Keating-Velasco

If your child has special dietary needs, be sure to send something for her to enjoy during school parties. Eating is a social time, and you don't want your child to miss out on the interaction.
Teresa Cardon

Practice egg hunts for Easter at home first. Put items in plastic eggs that motivate your child. It doesn't matter what it is (paper clips, stickers, candy, etc.), you just want your child to get excited about opening the egg. Bring some of your child's special eggs to the "real" egg hunt in case she can't have or isn't interested in the eggs at the event.
Chari Reynolds

If your child loves the colors and designs that fireworks make, but the noise is too loud, provide earplugs. If the noise level is still too loud, watch from a distance. Fireworks can be seen and still enjoyed from miles away.
Amy Bixler Coffin

For Halloween, let your child pick the costume. Go to the store when it's not busy and follow her around. See what interests her. If she doesn't want to wear a costume, that's okay, too.
Joanna Keating-Velasco

Have the child practice wearing small pieces of the costume days before the actual event. Start with a cape or wings, then a few days later add the headpiece, and so on. Take baby steps. Ultimately, let the child wear what she is comfortable with for parties and trick or treating – the ultimate goal is the fun, social aspect of the holiday.
Teresa Cardon

If the child doesn't want to visit Santa or the Easter Bunny, don't!
Joanna Keating-Velasco

It is soooooo hard to wait to open gifts on Christmas morning! Create a turn-taking card* to help your child know when it is his turn to open a gift. When he is handed the turn-taking card, it is his turn. When the card is handed to someone else, it is the child's turn to wait.
Amy Bixler Coffin

Wrap up 24 holiday books or special stuffed animals and starting on December 1 let your child open one present every day until Christmas. It doubles as a great advent calendar, too.
Teresa Cardon

Holiday Dinners

1 Find ways to add structure to what are often confusing and overwhelming events. Give the child something to do. For example, assign him the job of handing out place cards to the guests as they arrive.
Stephen Shore

2 Tradition is what your family makes it! Don't expect the child to sit through a noisy dining-room gathering for an hour. Plan to rotate group time with quiet time. Allow the child to go to a quiet area and come back occasionally to rejoin the group. Don't expect any more than usual just because it's a holiday.
Joanna Keating-Velasco

3 Hire a favorite babysitter (one your child is already familiar with) to come to the holiday dinner and help entertain the kids while the adults eat. The children can eat later when the grown-ups are finished and there are more hands to help out. That way everyone can enjoy the dinner.
Joanna Keating-Velasco

4 Have kid-friendly food available. You may want to use a First/Then* card to initiate trying the holiday food, then give the kid-friendly option.
Joanna Keating-Velasco

5 Put a little bit of everything on the child's plate, including many desirable foods. Watch what she tries. If there is a "repulsive" food on the plate, remove it, because it's her holiday too!!
Joanna Keating-Velasco

Set up a separate children's table in another room. Perhaps several teenage relatives won't mind rotating and being in charge of the kids for a short period of time. This will enable you to enjoy your holiday dinner.
Joanna Keating-Velasco

If possible, find special plates (something to match the holiday with special colors and characters) to help your child understand the concept of a special meal.
Joanna Keating-Velasco

Holiday dinners and parties insinuate a lot of people in a party atmosphere, which could mean sensory overload. Make sure to provide a BREAK card* for your child. Practice using it with her ahead of the event and provide a calming place to take the break (a small supervised wading pool or quiet movie environment), every time she gives you the card.
Joanna Keating-Velasco

Help your child learn to understand social boundaries – when children can/should enter adult conversations, appropriate topics to bring up, voice volume, etc. Develop hand signals as a way of letting your child know she needs to check herself. Hand signals can tell your child to stop talking, speak in a quieter voice, or come sit by mom or dad so you can have a quick whisper-chat to explain things she's missing. Have a discussion in the car on the way to the family gathering as a reminder of what's appropriate and what's not. The same rules and hand signals can apply to everyone in the family. This helps your child understand that these are social rules for everyone, not just specific challenges for her.
Kathryn Jolley

Keep slips of paper in a bowl that list your child's favorite topics, family memories, favorite movies, etc. Occasionally, have a person at the dinner table choose a slip of paper and ask everyone to take turns talking about the topic. Your child will have an interest in the topics since you have pre-selected the topics to be of interest to him. Be sure to coach your child to stay on topic and offer support when needed.
Teresa Cardon

CHAPTER 9

All the Rest ...

This chapter covers important topics that should not be overlooked. Many of the tips included here can be effective supports for the topics discussed in previous chapters. So think about integrating the ideas you read here in a variety of situations and locations.

Support Groups

1 Parents of other children on the autism spectrum are your best allies and sources of information. We live in the "trenches" every day and come to understand our children better than any expert ever will. Find a good support group, in person or online, and then hang on for dear life when you need to. There are all kinds of groups; if you don't like the first one you try, ask around and keep going until you find a good fit.
Melissa Van Hook

2 If you want to start a support group, put advertisements for your group in every free local and community paper – Moms' Clubs, church clubs, school newspapers, etc. Leave flyers in doctor's offices, therapy centers and preschools (ask for permission before you leave fliers anywhere). Never put your address on the flyers. Also, it is better to use a cell phone number than a home phone number, as it is less traceable.
Cindy O'Dell

3 A casual meeting at the park with other moms can turn into a great support group. Mothers can feel comfortable sharing in an open setting and their kids can play on the playground in the meantime.
Cindy O'Dell

4 Pick a certain day of the month to attend support group meetings. It will make it easier for you to remember and you are more likely to go if you have child care lined up.
Cindy O'Dell

Support groups are important because they allow you to meet and sit among others who feel the same hurt and frustrations you feel. Knowing you are not alone is a must. There is incredible comfort in being with others who really understand your daily grind.
Cindy O'Dell

Support groups are great places to find out which agencies might have openings for therapy or what therapists work well with children on the spectrum. Support groups are also great places to find out who provides good haircuts, what doctors and dentists work best with children on the spectrum and lots of other insider details.
Teresa Cardon

Support groups offer great opportunities for networking and information sharing and gathering. You get very helpful tips on new doctors, medications, programs, etc. You learn a lot in a short amount of time.
Cindy O'Dell

Support groups can be great places to trade books, materials, toys, sensory activities, etc. Swapping with other moms who have already tried things out brings a wealth of practical knowledge to any group.
Teresa Cardon

Dads need support groups, too. Time for dads to get together and just hang out with other men who are experiencing similar family dynamics can be very helpful. Maybe "meetings" can take place at a bowling alley or a driving range. Remember, the benefit of getting together is still there, even if it doesn't look like a traditional support group.
Teresa Cardon

If you aren't ready to attend a full-blown support group, at least try to find a couple of other parents to exchange phone numbers with or meet at a park on occasion. A diagnosis of autism is a long and winding journey, and not one that should be traveled alone.
Teresa Cardon

Visual Supports

Create a picture schedule of all your child's therapists. This is great for helping with all the transitions throughout the day.
Terri Anasagasti

Create a visual schedule* using pictures or words to help your child know what to expect throughout the day. Keep it in a central location, like the kitchen or by the garage door.
Teresa Cardon

Create a First/Then board* at home. Use it during meals, play time, therapy time, etc. If you are consistent, your child will become familiar with how it works. The goal is to teach your child the concept behind the words "first" and "then" so that she will eventually be able to understand it without the board.
Teresa Cardon

Create positive associations with visual supports by pairing favorite items and activities with the visual support when it is first introduced. Children are much more likely to be excited about something that is fun and motivating than something that seems like a punishment or chore. For example, a choice board* should include all of your child's favorite toys the first few times you use it.
Teresa Cardon

When using visual supports to teach your child, hand the child the visual. Don't just hold it up for him to look at. This helps him learn through another modality (other than hearing) and allows him some control over his communication because he can point to or pull off the picture he is interested in.
Chari Reynolds

Even if the child is verbal, she will still benefit from visual supports. Visual supports can help with just about anything. So, if your child is struggling with an activity, find a way to make it visual. For example, if your child is having a hard time learning how to transition from one activity to the next, create a card that states "all done". Each time he sees it, it will help to signify a change in activities. Or if your child is having a hard time waiting for his turn on the swings, visually show him with a timer how long he has to wait. It decreases ambiguity and can save a lot of frustration and confusion for everyone.
Teresa Cardon

The use of commercial picture cards with random pictures of other children may not work for your child. Take pictures of your child, laminate them and put them in a binder that therapists can use to teach sequencing. For example, to figure out the steps to brushing his teeth, use picture cards showing your child brushing his teeth: putting the toothpaste on the brush, brushing his teeth, rinsing, etc. You can use this strategy for many things such as getting in the car, getting dressed, and eating at the table. If your child is struggling with those tasks, the binder is a good reminder of what to do.
Cindy O'Dell

Purchase a laminator. It is worth every penny. When you take the time to take pictures for visual supports, laminate them so they last longer and can be used over and over again!
Cindy O'Dell

Purchase a digital camera that also takes video and that fits in your purse. Pull it out at any time and video when your child is doing something that you want his therapists to see: when you are having a specific problem or when he is doing well. The videos also provide feedback for the child. For example, you can videotape him playing with a friend, going to the doctor, etc., and then watch it afterwards. You can discuss things like "what were you doing?" "where were you?" or "how did you feel?"
Cindy O'Dell

When you see small photo albums in the dollar section of a store, stock up! They are just the right size to make the personalized stories* you create for your child portable. Take pictures for dentist trips, trips to the grocery store, trips to the park, what to expect on play dates, etc. Use sticky labels on the bottom of the pictures as a space to write out the story. Soon you will have your own library of visual supports that you can read often with your child.

Teresa Cardon

Sensory Suggestions

1 At bedtime, try deep pressure. For example, roll the child up tightly in a blanket like a "burrito." Or use a weighted blanket.
Melissa Van Hook

2 During the day, if the child gets too wound up, be ready with activities at home to meet her needs (i.e., things to satisfy proprioceptive [unconscious awareness of movement and spatial orientation within the body; awareness of the position of one's body] and tactile [touch] senses). For example, to help regulate the proprioceptive system, try having the child bounce on a trampoline, swing, spin (in a desk chair, if that is what happens to be available), or swim. To help with some tactile sensory needs, try chewing (gum, taffy, gummy bears, or chewy tubes); digging in sand, rice, dried beans (these last two can be kept in a big plastic tub with a lid); or maybe playing with play dough, Moonsand (see Appendix), or clay.
Melissa Van Hook

3 Learn to recognize when your child is "maxed out" and respect that she is becoming short-tempered, agitated, anxious or fearful. Act quickly. If you are out in public and it is possible to go home, do so. (Many things can wait until another day, and if your child has a full-blown meltdown because her limits were not recognized and respected, it is a miserable experience for both parent and child.) If you cannot leave, try to go somewhere quiet to give your child a chance to recover. If you are at home with guests present, or at a family gathering at someone else's home, take the child to a quiet part of the house and let her engage

in a favorite soothing activity. She may only need 15 minutes or so by herself and then be ready to participate again. Tuning in to your child's needs can salvage an entire day, and it can allow your whole family to be a part of "normal" activities.
Melissa Van Hook

Do not be embarrassed or ashamed of your child's sensory differences; you do not have to explain or justify to anybody your actions to take care of your child. Try to be respectful of others around you, but beyond that, just do your best. Get over the fear of being stared at or making a scene. If you must say something to that nosy busy-body giving you the death glare that screams, "Spank that bratty child!," simply smile sweetly and say, "We are having a rough day; autism can be very challenging at times."
Melissa Van Hook

Reduce visual stimulation in the child's working environment (walls, desk). Avoid seating him by windows, doors or walkways.
Jenny Clark Brack

Provide a cozy corner with pillows and low light where the child can read or retreat when over-stimulated.
Jenny Clark Brack

Exposure, exposure, exposure! As difficult, embarrassing, and even painful as it can be, sometimes the more you expose your child to things that he is having a hard time with, the more he will adjust to them over time.
Cindy O'Dell

Purchase a small wading pool and bring it indoors. Fill it with beans, rice, sand, feathers, pasta, or whatever else you think your child might like. It is a great way to experiment with different textures. (You might want to put a vinyl tablecloth under the wading pool because it is going to get messy.)
Teresa Cardon

9 If your child is hypo-sensitive to movement, buy toys that provide a lot of sensory input. Swings, trampolines, Sit-N-Spins, roller boards, etc., can be great tools to help get your child's sensory system in check by providing the extra movement input that she is seeking.
Teresa Cardon

10 Create a "cozy corner" somewhere in your house with lots of blankets, beanbags, pillows, stuffed animals, etc. Your child can find comfort in a quiet space that is calming.
Teresa Cardon

10 Extra Tips

Some tips didn't seem to fit anywhere else – but they were so great we wanted to find a place for them. Read on for some extra special advice!

1 When choosing or helping your child select clothes at the store, be sure to look at current fashion and how it's worn. Kids who are dressed in a fashion similar to the norm don't draw attention to themselves. Kids who dress noticeably out of fashion have just added to their social difficulties through their attire. Whether we like it or not, "un-cool" style is a social faux pas in any school.
Joan Clark

2 To help vitamins go down, cut them in half. You can also put supplements in juice or peanut butter to help them go down easier.
Terri Anasagasti

3 For a young girl starting her period, take her to the store and let her pick out two identical special bags for her personal items – one for school and one for home. Create a picture or word chart for each step in the changing pad process. Place this in the bag with an extra pair of underwear, pads and wipes. You may want to place an "I Need Help"* card in there also for her to request assistance.
Joanna Keating-Velasco

4 Big or small college? Choosing a place of higher education for a college-bound student with ASD is the same as it is for everyone else, but there is one additional facet. It is important to interview

126

the office of disabilities and ask questions like, "Can this office and the school as a whole provide the needed support for the person on the autism spectrum?" Colleges and universities are in the business of education. They are not rehabilitative institutions. This means that higher education may not be appropriate for a given young person at a particular time.
Stephen Shore

Death is very difficult to explain to anyone, including children on the spectrum. Your child may become angry and display verbal aggression at the death of a close family member or friend. Your child needs closure, particularly if there is only a memorial service and no burial. It may help to find a show or movie about death and burial.* Your child needs to understand that it isn't his fault and that the loved one can't come back.
Susan Morris

Find a reliable family member, neighbor or a neighbor's teenage child who is willing and excited to establish a relationship with your child. There will be times when you need help, and having a neighbor who is familiar with your child will alleviate a lot of pressure. You can use this person as a baby sitter or just someone who can step in when you need a break. It is important to find this person and establish a relationship with him or her before you need help at the last minute.
Teresa Cardon

There is so much information about ASD out there that it is hard to know what interventions and approaches you should think about for your child. There are several questions you can ask yourself before you decide to start a new intervention.
    1. Is it research based?
    2. Does it feel safe and make sense to me?
    3. Does the cost seem astronomical?
    4. Is there a trained professional guiding the treatment?
    5. Am I changing approaches so often that nothing has
       been given adequate time to make a difference?
Teresa Cardon

Teach your child about personal safety. Consider skills such as knowing who to hug and kiss and when it is more appropriate to shake hands, how to discretely carry money, NOT giving personal information to others over the Internet, and what to do if you are walking down the street and someone unfamiliar approaches you or you feel that you are being followed.
Diane Adreon

At mealtimes, talk, talk, talk – and talk some more. Start with simple games like, "I'm thinking of someone who is wearing a red shirt" and ask the child to guess who at the table is wearing a red shirt. Every night pick different attributes and describe everyone around the table.
Cindy O'Dell

Join an organization like www.freecycle.org . They offer free items in your area like mini-trampolines, bikes, balls, etc. Many of these are terrific for use in the classroom or in your home As free items come up, you can ask your child's teacher if he would like them donated to the classroom.
Joanna Keating-Velasco

Final Thoughts

I hope you have found many of the tips in this book helpful to you and your family. It truly has been a labor of love, and many amazing people have contributed their thoughts and ideas. My sincerest thanks! It is inspiring to see what we can do when we come together as an autism community.

Be sure to check out the Appendix for helpful resources, including a list of the books and websites that are mentioned throughout the book. The top 10 lists of books and other resources were selected based on input from colleagues, parents, and others who have found these resources helpful in their work with or parenting of a child on the autism spectrum. I recognize that your top ten lists may be different, as no two children with autism spectrum disorders or their families are alike. Try the new lists out and add to or delete from your own lists of favorites. The Appendix also provides more details about the strategies throughout the book marked with an asterisk.

One book of tips can never encompass all of the amazing ideas and expertise that families and professionals have discovered. In fact, I'll bet that while reading this book you thought of many of your own ideas. Your ideas and strategies can help create the next "tip" book, so please send them to me at teresa.cardon@gmail.com. A strategy you use with your child every day may turn out to be a novel way to help someone else.

APPENDIX

Autism Blogs

http://autism.about.com/b/ – Lisa Jo Rudy is the mother of Tommy, age 11, diagnosed with PDD-NOS – an autism spectrum disorder. She is also a professional writer, researcher, and consultant with nearly 20 years of experience in science education and science writing.

http://www.translatingautism.com/ – Nestor L. Lopez-Duran, Ph.D., is a clinical child psychologist and neuroscience researcher working at a large midwest university-based child psychiatric institute. He conducts studies on affect regulation and mood disorders in children and adolescents. He is also the founder of the Translating Research Project, a series of informational blogs designed to rapidly disseminate scientific research findings in neurological and psychiatric childhood disorders and translate these findings into information useful to parents, educators, and clinicians. Translating Autism, the first blog of this project, was launched in January of 2008.

http://www.autismvox.com/ – Kristina Chew is the mother of Charlie, her son who has autism. She is called every day to translate his sometimes garbled speech and his needs. She is called to action and to advocate, and she believes that blogging on Autism Vox will help to spread the word.

http://www.geocities.com/autistry/oddizms.html – This is a blog for people and families living with autism put together by autistics. This blog explores why autistics probably don't really want to cure autism now.

Choice board – A visual way of showing a child what choices are available at a given time. Pictures or drawings may be used to ensure comprehension, in addition to or in lieu of words.

After School I Can:

| Jump on the trampoline | Watch my favorite TV program | Play on the computer |

Circle of friends – A program to support children who are having difficulty making friends. A facilitator supports a child with ASD and typical peers as they develop friendships and learn to interact socially with one another. For more details, see *With Open Arms* by M. Schlieder (Autism Asperger Publishing Company, 2007; www.asperger.net).

Countdown – Visual way of showing the amount of time that is left for a given activity; particularly helpful to ease waiting. Gradually remove or cross out the next highest number in the sequence until all of the numbers are gone.

Cue card – Communication supports that provide a visual of what to say or how to behave in certain situations. May also be used with children who are unable to formulate verbal responses due to anxiety in novel or uncomfortable situations.

Sample Cue Card

Rules for the Library

1. Use an inside voice.

2. Don't run.

3. Look only at one book at a time.

4. Be sure to put books that you are not checking out back where they belong.

Death – Resources for Helping Children Cope

http://www.nas.org.uk/nas/jsp/polopoly.jsp?d=528&a=15957 – This webpage from the National Autistic Society has some good strategies to help individuals with autism understand death.

Several other resources can be helpful when trying to talk about and explain burial, cremation and death. The following books are not specifically written for people with ASD, but they contain many pictures and are, therefore, ideal for use with individuals who have autism.

Mansfield, M., et al. (2006). *When Someone Dies: Written and Designed by People with Learning Difficulties*. Cambridge, UK: Speaking Up. (www.speakingup.org)

Hollins, S., Blackman, N., & Dowling, S. (2003). *Books Beyond Words: When Somebody Dies*. London: The Royal College of Psychiatrists and St. George's Hospital Medical School. (www.rcpsych.ac.uk/publications/booksbeyondwords/bbw/1901242900.aspx)

Hollins, S., Sireling, L., & Webb, B. (2004). *Books Beyond Words: When Mum Died*. London: The Royal College of Psychiatrists and St. George's Hospital Medical School. (www.rcpsych.ac.uk/publications/booksbeyondwords/bbw/1904671039.aspx)

Hollins, S., Sireling, L., & Webb, B. (2004). *Books Beyond Words: When Dad Died*. London: The Royal College of Psychiatrists and St. George's Hospital Medical School. (www.rcpsych.ac.uk/publications/booksbeyondwords/bbw/1904671047.aspx)

First/Then card/board – A simple, yet highly effective visual support. Take a small piece of foam board and draw a line down the center. The word "first" goes to the left of the line and the word "then" goes to the right of the line. You can put actual objects on the board to show a child what will happen first and what will happen second or you can take pictures of activities and toys and place them on the board.

5-point scale – This easily adaptable scale can turn social and emotional situations that are difficult for the child into a concrete, visual number system to which she can more easily relate. Make with input from the child. (For more information, see *The Incredible 5-Point Scale*, Buron & Curtis, 2004. Shawnee Mission, KS: Autism Asperger Publishing company; www.asperger.net).

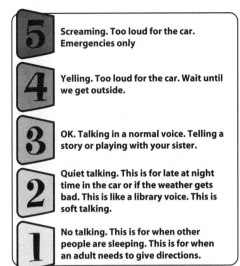

5 Screaming. Too loud for the car. Emergencies only

4 Yelling. Too loud for the car. Wait until we get outside.

3 OK. Talking in a normal voice. Telling a story or playing with your sister.

2 Quiet talking. This is for late at night time in the car or if the weather gets bad. This is like a library voice. This is soft talking.

1 No talking. This is for when other people are sleeping. This is for when an adult needs to give directions.

I need help/I need a break card – A card with a picture and words indicating that a child needs help with a particular activity or a brief break. The child usually needs to be prompted on how to effectively use the card multiple times before he is able to use it independently.

I NEED A BREAK

Introductory sample letter for Scout leaders, coaches, etc.

Our Child on the Autism Spectrum*

Date:

Hello, we are *child's name* parents. Our child has been diagnosed with an autism spectrum disorder (ASD), which is a neurobiological and developmental disorder effecting many areas of his life. Children with autism have difficulty communicating, using and understanding nonverbal behaviors, and developing peer relationships. While they often have specific interests and skills in certain areas, they may have a great deal of difficulty with organization. Children with autism often have difficulty with sensory issues and very strongly rely on routine.

You will learn that *child's name* has many strengths. However, listed below are some issues that may become apparent to you as you work with *child's name*. Many of the behaviors that may puzzle you are NOT under his control and are NOT a result of willful misbehavior. At times *child's name* does not instinctively know how to respond. The following are some areas to watch out for and some simple strategies and suggestions for how to support and help him. Please call us at any time if you have questions about our child or about autism. We can be reached at:

Names _____ Phone Numbers _____

General Behaviors
- The autism spectrum is characterized by a sort of "swiss cheese" type of development. That is, children with autism spectrum disorders learn some things in pretty much the same way and at the same time as other kids, but may lag behind in other areas or lack certain skills altogether.
- It is important to remember that just because the child learns something in one situation, it doesn't automatically mean that she will remember or will be able to generalize the learning to new situations.
- Our child reacts well to positive and patient styles of teaching.
- Generally speaking, it is more effective if you use a calm voice rather than raising your voice or repeating commands over and over again in rapid-fire succession.

- At times, our child may experience "meltdowns" when nothing seems to help his behavior. At these times, please allow a "safe and quiet spot" where he can go to "cool off." Try to take note of what occurred before the meltdown (change in routine, loud noises, etc.) and always wait to discuss the situation until well after he has calmed down.
- When you see anger or other outbursts, our child is not being deliberately difficult. Instead this is a "fight/fright/flight" reaction to a hard situation.
- Our child may need help in problem-solving situations. Please be willing to take the time to help with this. If you are willing to be patient, he may just surprise you with what he comes up with.
- Note his strengths often and visually. This will give our child the courage to keep on trying.
- Foster an environment that supports the acceptance of differences and diversity. I am more than willing to come in and do a short presentation to the children to explain some of these differences. I can read a short story, guide a discussion about it, and then answer any questions the students may have. Please let me know if you are interested.

Repeating Things/Perseverations
- Our child may repeat or do the same thing over and over again, and you may find this increases as his stress or anxiety increases.
- It can be helpful to redirect the repetitive behavior to something more appropriate or help him find another way to deal with the stress or anxiety.

Transitions
- Our child has difficulty with transitions. Having a picture or word schedule may help.
- Please try to give as much advance notice as possible if there is going to be a change or disruption in the schedule. He can learn to adapt to change, but only if given enough time to shift gears.
- Giving one or two warnings before a change of activity may also be helpful.

Sensory
- Our child may get overstimulated by loud noises and/or bright lights because of his heightened sensitivity to these things.
- He is especially sensitive to loud sounds like other children crying and the fire alarm. Please allow him to find a comfortable place

away from the noise until it stops. Advanced warning helps him to deal more appropriately with these situations.

- If there is going to be lots of other kids, chaos, and noise, our child may need to find a quiet spot where he can go to "get away."
- Unstructured times (like between activities and during breaks) are often the most difficult for him. Please try to help provide some guidance and extra adults to redirect if necessary during these more difficult times.
- Allow him to "move around" as sitting still for long periods of time can be very difficult (even a 5 minute walk around with a friend or an aide can help a lot; send him on errands around the building). He often has trouble staying seated during class, but can do fairly well if allowed to stand to do his work at times.

Listening Skills
- Our child has difficulty understanding a series of steps or directions or too many words at one time.
- Try breaking down directions into smaller, simpler steps for him to follow.
- Using picture cues or short, simple directions may also help. It may help to give hand signals to reinforce certain directions like "stop," "wait your turn" or "come with me".
- Try to speak slower and in smaller phrases for him to understand.
- Directions are more easily understood if they are repeated clearly and simply.
- Try not to repeat a direction unless you know he did not hear you as it takes him a few moments to process what was asked of him and then take action. If you repeat a direction he will have to process it again and will take even longer to do what is being asked of him.
- At times, it may take more than a few seconds for my child to respond to questions. He needs to stop what he's thinking, put that somewhere, formulate an answer, and then respond. Please wait patiently for the answer and encourage others to do the same. Otherwise he will have to start this whole process over again.
- When someone tries to help by finishing his sentences or interrupting, he often has to go back and start over to get his train of thought back.

Language
- Although his vocabulary and use of language may seem high, he may not always know the meaning of what he is saying even though the words sound correct. Occasionally ask him the meaning of some of the words he says to check his comprehension.
- Sarcasm and some forms of humor are often not understood by my child. He is very literal and takes everything at its at face value, so be careful that he understands the true meaning of your words if you are joking or being sarcastic.

Routine
- A consistent routine is very important to most children with autism, but can be very difficult to maintain on a regular basis. Our child likes to be able to count on nothing out of the ordinary changing for him so he knows how to react in each situation.
- Please let our child know of any anticipated changes as soon as you know them, especially on his picture or word schedule.

Organizational Skills
- Our child lacks the ability to remember a lot of information or how to retrieve that information for his use. Schedules help keep him on track.
- Please post activities or other project schedules for him to see and also make sure he has a copy.
- Please make sure that any assignments or instructions go home with him; he can't always be counted on to get everything home without help. E-mailing us is a great way to communicate.
- Many children with autism are unable to listen to you, talk, read the board, and take notes at the same time. Please be aware of these limitations for him and adjust your expectations accordingly.

Eye Contact
- At times, it may look like my child is not listening to you when he really is. Don't assume that because he is not looking at you that he is not hearing you. Please do not force him to look at you as this is hard for him.
- Unlike most of us, sometimes forcing eye contact BREAKS his concentration.
- He may actually hear and understand you better if not forced to look directly at your eyes.

Social Skills and Friendships
- This area can be one of the biggest challenges for children with autism. They may want to make friends, yet not know what steps to take to make it happen.
- Identifying a couple of willing students who can serve as "buddies" may help him feel more comfortable and feel that he has friends,
- Talking with the class/team about the importance of friendship and how we can all be friendly to one another even if we are not all the same can go a long way towards tolerance and acceptance.
- It may be helpful to discuss how we all have challenges in different areas (like needing glasses/hearing aids) and the child with autism is challenged to understand friend relationships as well.
- Children with autism are at greater risk for becoming victims of bullying by other children. Children with autism want to be liked so badly that they are reluctant to tell on the bully for fear of rejection from the other students. Please keep a close eye on how the other children are treating him, especially during unstructured time, as this is when bullying situations arise the most frequently.

We invite you to communicate with us whenever you wish. The more open we are with each other, the faster we will be able to resolve any issues that may arise. Communication is the key, and by working together we can make this a successful experience for everyone. Thank you for your willingness to support our child.

Thank you very much,

Parent Names
*contributed by Katie Wride and Sharon Hayes.

Personalized story – Story written about an upcoming event/experience. Personal stories help prepare children for changes and new events. For example, if the child is about to go on an airplane, a personal story about what will happen on the airplane would be appropriate. Adjust the language and choice of illustrations to the child's age and level of functioning.

When we go to grandma's next week, we will be taking an airplane. We will have to get up early in the morning and drive to the airport. After we park the car, we will take a small bus to the airport building. There we will have to stand in line to check in and give them our suitcases (we get them back when we land again). Then we have to wait for a while in the airport before we get on the plane. We will be sure you bring something to read and music to listen to. Also, we will bring a snack and get something to drink. Etc. Etc.

Power Card – Cards that use the child's special interest as a motivator to provide her with information she needs to make good decisions about new situations or environments (for more information, see *Power cards: Using special interests to motivate children and youth with Asperger Syndrome and Autism*, E. Gagnon, 2001; Shawnee Mission, KS: Autism Asperger Publishing Company; www.asperger.net).

Sam

Sam is a highly intelligent sixth-grade student with a diagnosis of Asperger Syndrome. Sam hopes one day to attend Harvard and often speaks of this plan to anyone willing to listen. But even though Sam is intelligent, he has developed few organizational strategies. Specifically, he doesn't ask questions about course requirements and therefore often fails to turn in assignments on time. The following scenario and POWER CARD were introduced to Sam by his mother to provide him with organizational strategies.

1. Take class notes and write all assignments in a calendar.

2. Ask questions when you don't understand.

3. Break down assignments into small steps, assign deadlines for each step, and write all deadlines and assignment due dates in a calendar.

Copyright 2001 by President and Fellows of Harvard College. Used with permission.

From: *Power cards: Using special interests to motivate children and youth with Asperger Syndrome and Autism*, E. Gagnon, 2001. Shawnee Mission, KS: Autism Asperger Publishing Company; www.asperger.net. Reprinted with permission.

Rebus symbols – Picture symbols that often accompany words in sentences or phrases to add a visual representation of the word to help the child understand the sentence.

FAMILY

Reward chart – A visual support to depict how well a child is doing on his way to receiving an award. Reward charts often have rows of squares that you can place stickers, check marks, or smiley faces in to indicate what a child has earned. When a sticker or mark is placed in the final box, the child has earned a pre-determined award.

REWARD CHART

Place token here	Place token here	Place token here

Working For:
Computer Time

Sequence chart – A visual depiction of a sequence of events. May be for short sequences such as hand washing or longer sequences such as an entire day's schedule.

From: *Making visual supports work in the home and community: Strategies for individuals with autism and Asperger Syndrome,* J. L. Savner & B. S. Myles (2000). Shawnee Mission, KS: Autism Asperger Publishing Company; www.asperger.net. Reprinted with permission.

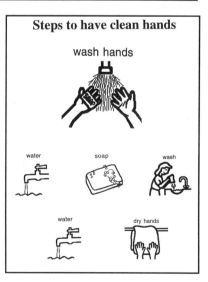

Steps to have clean hands

wash hands

water   soap   wash

water   dry hands

Turn-taking card – A card listing pictures or names of children playing a game. The card is turned to indicate whose turn is next in the game.

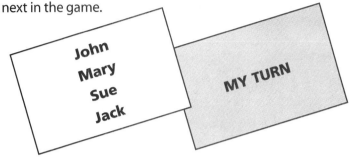

Visual recipe – Provides pictures of each step of a procedure, event, etc., so that the child can see a given process from start to finish. If doing a craft, create it ahead of time and take pictures as you go. Number each picture from start to finish and describe each step that is being implemented. Once your child has completed the task, you can use the visual recipe as a sequencing activity. Help the child put the steps in order and then talk about the activity in the past tense. Mix the steps up and let the child put them in the right order on her own.

1. Get out felt pieces and scissors.
2. Cut out felt along the marked line.
3. Get out string.
4. Cut string in five 10 inch pieces.
Etc.

Visual schedule – Way of presenting a sequence of events/activities for a certain period of time in a visual format.

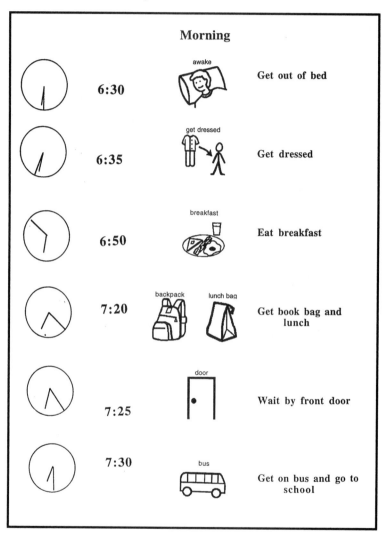

From: *Making visual supports work in the home and community: Strategies for individuals with autism and Asperger Syndrome,* J. L. Savner & B.S. Myles, 2000. Shawnee Mission, KS: Autism Asperger Publishing Company; www.asperger.net. Reprinted with permission.

Top 10 Books for School Support and IEPs

1. Aspy, R., & Grossman, B. (2007). *The Ziggurat Model.* Shawnee Mission, KS: Autism Asperger Publishing Company.
   This book presents a process and framework for designing comprehensive interventions for individuals of all ages with autism spectrum disorders. The Ziggurat Model was designed to simplify a complex process. Parents and professionals will find the framework of the Ziggurat Model to be a guide in developing more thorough and effective interventions.

2. Brewer, R. D., & Mueller, T. G. (2008). *Strategies at Hand: Quick and Handy Strategies for Working with Students on the Autism Spectrum.* Shawnee Mission, KS: Autism Asperger Publishing Company.
   This at-your-fingertips tool reintroduces the much-valued concept of convenience to parents, teachers, paraprofessionals, and related professionals who work with students with autism spectrum disorders. It features easy-to-implement strategies that can be used in all types of educational settings and situations.

3. Cohen, J. (2006). *Guns A' Blazing.* Shawnee Mission, KS: Autism Asperger Publishing Company.
   This book offers helpful and balanced advice to parents on how to get the best possible services for their children without resorting to undue controversy.

4. Henry. S., & Myles, B. (2007). *The Comprehensive Autism Planning System (CAPS) for Individuals with Asperger Syndrome, Autism and Related Disabilities: Integrating Best Practices Throughout the Student's Day.* Shawnee Mission, KS: Autism Asperger Publishing Company.
   This comprehensive, yet easy-to-use system allows educators to understand how and when to implement an instructional program for students with autism spectrum disorders.

Kluth P. (2004). *Your Gonna Love This Kid!* Baltimore: Brookes
  Publishing.
  This is a practical book for the classroom that begins
  with accounts of those who have lived and experienced
  educating individuals with autism and what their experiences can tell us about creating inclusive classroom
  environments that work.

Myles, B. (2005). *Children and Youth With Asperger Syndrome: Strategies for Success in Inclusive Settings.* Shawnee Mission,
  KS: Autism Asperger Publishing Company.
  This book provides important strategies in teaching
  children and youth diagnosed with Asperger Syndrome.
  This essential resource for teachers and other educators
  presents research-based, instructional, behavioral, and
  environmental strategies for teachers.

Prizant, B., Wetherby, A., Rubin, E., Rydell, P., & Laurent, A. (2006).
  *The SCERTS Model: A Comprehensive Educational Ap-
  proach for Children with Autism Spectrum Disorders.*
  Baltimore: Brookes Publishing.
  The SCERTS® Model is a comprehensive educational approach and multidisciplinary framework that addresses
  the core challenges faced by children with autism
  spectrum disorder and related disabilities. The model is
  derived from a theoretical as well as a research-based
  foundation on communication and social-emotional development in children with and without special needs.

Twachtman-Cullen, D. (2000). *How to Be a Para Pro: A Comprehensive Training Manual for Paraprofessionals.* Higganum, CT:
  Starfish Specialty Press.
  This user-friendly training manual is divided into two
  parts. Part One is a "short course" on autism spectrum
  disorders (ASD) for people "in the trenches." Part Two
  takes a "cookbook style" look at the art and science of
  paraprofessional support for students with ASD and
  those with other cognitive impairments.

Weiss, M. J. (2008). *Practical Solutions for Educating Young Children with High-Functioning Autism and Asperger Syndrome.* Shawnee Mission, KS: Autism Asperger Publishing Company. This book is designed to help parents and professionals navigate the challenges for early learners with high-functioning autism (HFA) and Asperger Syndrome (AS). Because their deficits are more subtle, these children may be less understood by educational professionals. This book is a much-needed resource to help teachers understand their younger child with HFA or AS.

Wright, W. D., & Wright, P. (2007). *Wrightslaw: Special Education Law, 2nd Edition.* Hartfield, VA: Harbor House Law Press. This book is an invaluable resource that provides a clear roadmap to the laws surrounding special education.

Top 10 Peer Support and Demystification Tools

Cardon, R., & Cardon, T. (2007). *What I Have Learned About Autism: A Second Grader's Interpretation.* www.lulu.com. This book was written and illustrated by a second grader and is an excellent tool to help children understand autism.

Keating-Velasco, J. (2007). *A Is for Autism, F Is for Friend.* Shawnee Mission, KS: Autism Asperger Publishing Company. This book provides a unique glimpse of life from the perspective of a child who has severe autism.

Larson, E. (2006). *I Am Utterly Unique.* Shawnee Mission, KS: Autism Asperger Publishing Company. This book, laid out in an A-to-Z format, celebrates the extraordinary gifts and unique perspectives that children with ASD possess. Each page of this playful alphabet book presents one of the children's many talents and abilities. The kid-friendly illustrations and clever text create a positive portrayal of children with ASD.

Lowell, J. & Tuchel, T. (2005). *My Best Friend Will*. Shawnee Mission, KS: Autism Asperger Publishing Company.
This book allows you to enter Willie's world through Jamie's eyes as it unfolds at school, at home, and at play. In the process, you will gain a rich understanding and appreciation of Willie's many unique qualities and come to accept that these are all a part of who he is.

Nick News: Private Worlds of Autism. http://video.aol.com video-detail/nick-news-private-worlds-kids-and-autism-full-length/423071765
This is a fantastic video that will help you educate children about autism. The family interviews provide unique insight and real everyday experiences.

Notbohm, E. (2005). *10 Things Every Child with Autism Wishes You Knew*. Arlington, TX: Future Horizons.
This book champions the cause of helping families discover the strengths of their child with autism. It validates everybody's capabilities and possibilities. It addresses early confrontations with "can't do" and redirects the focus onto what children "can do."

McCracken, H. (2006). *That's What's Different About Me! Helping Children Understand Autism Spectrum Disorders*. Shawnee Mission, KS: Autism Asperger Publishing Company.
The purpose of this program is to educate neurotypical children so that the child with autism spectrum disorders can assimilate into typical social situations.

McGinnity, K., & Neri, N. (2005). *Walk a While in My Autism*. Cambridge, MA: Cambridge Book Review Press.
This book is a manual of sensitivity presentations to promote understanding of people on the autism spectrum.

Sullivan, C., & Sullivan, D. (2001). *I Love My Brother! A Preschooler's View of Living with a Brother Who Has Autism*. Stratham, NH: PHATArt4.
This book is great for young siblings and is a nice guide for helping preschool and kindergarten-aged students better understand their peers with autism.

Wolfberg, P. (2005). *Peer Play and the Autism Spectrum: The Art of Guiding Children's Socialization and Imagination.* Shawnee Mission, Kansas: Autism Asperger Publishing Company. This practical guide offers an introduction to the basic principles, tools and techniques that comprise the Integrated Play Groups model, designed to support children of diverse ages and abilities on the autism spectrum (novice players) in mutually enjoyed play experiences with typical peers and siblings (expert players).

Top 10 Autism-Related Websites

www.foggyrock.com – This website is an autism group networking site where parents can connect with other parents.

http://www.talkaboutcuringautism.org/index.htm – The Talk About Curing Autism (TACA) website has great resources for parents with children who have been newly diagnosed.

www.dotolearn.com – This website has a great free section where you can download picture cards to use for visual schedules and choice boards. You can also subscribe for a nominal fee to use the entire site.

http://trainland.tripod.com – This website contains picture cards, schedules, autism articles, etc. It is a very helpful site in general.

www.pics4learning.com – This website contains thousands of free images (photographs and pictures) that you can use for visual supports.

www.autismshop.net – This is a great website to find toys, visual supports, and just about anything else to support individuals with autism. In fact, if they don't have it – it may not exist!!!!

www.discountschoolsupply.com – This is a site that carries great educational toys at a discounted price.

www.autism-society.org/ – The official website of the Autism Society of America.

www.autismspeaks.org – The Autism Speaks website.

www.autismhelp.info – A website with information about autism and autism resources.

Products

Leap Frog Videos – Talking Letter Factory & Talking Word Factory – www.leapfrog.com

Picture This [software] – www.silverliningmedia.com

Bop It – An electronic game from Hasbro. Available at major toy retailers.

Etch-a-Sketch – http://www.ohioart.com/etch Official website of Etch-a-sketch

Moonsand – Sand that molds like dough and never dries out; great to use indoors, available at moonsand.com or toy retailers.

Sit-N-Spin – A platform that children can sit on and spin. Available at major toy retailers.

Time Timer – A visual timer that counts down a set number of minutes using a red shaded area; www.timetimer.com

Autism Asperger Publishing Co.
P.O. Box 23173
Shawnee Mission, Kansas 66283-0173
www.asperger.net • 913-897-1004